DEPTH EXPLORATIONS IN THE NEW TESTAMENT

by

**Julius Robert Mantey,
Th.D., Ph.D., D.D.**

VANTAGE PRESS
New York / Washington / Atlanta
Los Angeles / Chicago

Published by Vantage Press, Inc.
516 West 34th Street, New York, New York 10001

Manufactured in the United States of America
Standard Book Number 533-04535-5

Library of Congress Catalog Card No.: 79-56511

Contents

Preface

During this generation, there has been a definite and wholesome trend toward biblical theology and research. At the turn of the century and for some decades afterward, the interest of biblical scholars was at times negative and quite speculative, emphasizing systematic rather than biblical theology. However, a new and a much more appreciative approach to the teachings of the Bible is now manifest. This can readily be noted through taking cognizance of the books coming off the press. It is apparent in the books that the World Council of Churches has been sponsoring. They are the findings of study groups (the author has been on one of them), appointed by the council for the purpose of ascertaining what the Bible has to say on vital, relevant issues and principles for our time.

In the program prepared for the 1954 Ecumenical Conference at Evanston, Illinois, during August, this statement occurred:

Realizing that a great deal has been accomplished in the exploration of differences and points of agreement between the churches, *it is now imperative* that the great discrepancy between unity in Christ and disunity in the churches be fully faced. This involves an assessment of the fullness of the church we have already been given; of the causes, both doctrinal and non-doctrinal, of our divisions; of the obedience demanded of us; and of the meaning for our disunity, which is contained in the judgment and hope of Christ.

Chapter 1

Too Much at Stake

The writer is author or coauthor of four books. One of them is *A Manual Grammar of the Greek New Testament,* which is the most widely used Greek grammar by ministers in the United States. Scores of his articles have appeared in scholarly journals and magazines. He has been president of the American Research Society and of the Biblical Research Society of Chicago, where he was professor of New Testament for thirty-five years at the Northern Baptist Theological Seminary.

Most people are going to be calling themselves fools during the endless years of eternity because they put off becoming Christians. Are *you* going to be one of them?

The Terrifying Fate of the Unredeemed

"Everyone who does what is sinful is of the devil" (1 John 3:8).

"You fool! This very night your life will be demanded from you. So is everyone who stores things up for himself and is not rich in relation to God" (Luke 12:20–21).

"Whoever does not obey the Son will not enjoy eternal life, for God's wrath remains on him" (John 3:36).

1

"They will go into eternal punishment" (Matt. 25:46).

"Having *no hope* and without God in the world" (Eph. 2:12).

"Not every one who says to me, 'Lord, Lord,' shall enter the kingdom of heaven, but *he who does the will of my Father* who is in heaven" (Matt. 7:21).

The Fantastic Future of the Redeemed

"Fear God and keep his commandments for this is the whole duty of man" (Eccles. 12:13).

"Seek *first* his kingdom and his righteousness and *all these things* shall be yours" (Matt. 6:33).

"We know that *all things* work together for good with those who love him" (Rom. 8:28).

"I came that they may have life and have it *abundantly*" (John 10:10).

"He *rejoiced* with all his family because he *had believed* in God" (Acts 16:34).

"Repent and be baptized *every one of you* in the name of Jesus Christ for the forgiveness of your sins; and *you will receive the gift of the Holy Spirit*" (Acts 2:38).

"The fruit of the Spirit is *love, joy, peace, patience, kindness, goodness, faithfulness, gentleness, self-control*" (Gal. 5:22–23).

"Surely goodness and mercy shall follow me *all the days* of my life, and I shall dwell in the house of the Lord *forever*" (Ps. 23:6).

Can any one afford not to have *such* a future?

THE WINTERS in Gannett, Idaho, are usually cold and empty enough. But when I was sixteen years old, my best girl friend gave me notice that we were "through." She said I had a bad reputation, and when I thought in contrast what a fine Christian girl I was losing, that winter was much colder and emptier than usual.

2

That parting night as I went home on horseback, I began to see myself for the first time as I really was and as others saw me. It was a sudden and severe shock to me. The more I thought about it, the more my pride became deflated.

A brother, four years older than I, had, with me, leased the family cattle ranch of 640 acres. We spent most of our time farming, "punching" cows, and in breaking broncos. Mother had bought from a colporteur a Bible, which gathered dust on a "parlor" shelf. I had never seen anyone read it, but mother used to hide money in it occasionally, confident that no one would ever look there. Since we had scarcely any other books, and feeling the need of something to occupy my mind and to help me to overcome the feeling of loneliness and frustration because my girl friend had "given me the gate," I smuggled that Bible upstairs to my room and began reading it secretly. Fortunately, I began with the book of Matthew, in the New Testament.

My whole life, because of that experience, suddenly and definitely was changed. I became impressed increasingly with the reasonableness and authority of the teachings of Christ, as I read chapter after chapter. But the real challenge to me came in Matt. 10:32, 33: "Every one therefore who shall confess Me before men, him will I also confess before My Father who is in Heaven. But whosoever shall deny Me before men, him I will also deny before My Father who is in Heaven." Here I was made aware that God's forgiveness was conditioned by my willingness, not only to repent of my sins and to live in full conformity with His will, but also by my readiness to let others know that I was a Christian.

As I went on reading, I came across this statement, where Jesus is speaking of His return to earth: "Then shall two men be in the field, one is taken, and one is left" (Matt. 24:40).

I was living in an environment in which it was exceedingly difficult to be a Christian. My people were not in the habit of going to church. We never had Bible reading or prayer in our home. The crowd I ran with were indifferent to Christianity, and we had habits that were definitely unchristian. As I thought therefore about confessing Christ, and as I recalled how my brother

3

and I worked together day after day in the field, and realizing that he was not a Christian, I feared that he would ridicule me, and others would call me a "sissy," in case I should take my stand openly for Christ. But as I thought of what Jesus had said, and as I realized that eternity lasts forever, whereas our life here on earth is exceedingly brief in comparison, and as I began to think of how unbearable and unspeakably tragic it would be in case I should lose out on having the favor of God forever and ever, because of my refusal to repent of my sins and to accept Christ as my Savior, I concluded that I could not afford not to accept Christ, for there was too much at stake. I realized that it would be infinitely better for me to have the ill-will and the ridicule of men all my life here rather than to have the disfavor of God hereafter.

So the most reasonable and the only logical thing left for me to do was to repent of my sins and to confess them to God and to ask Him for the sake of Christ to forgive and save me. I did not know how to pray, but I simply told God what I had decided to do and I asked Him to guide and help me to do it. Then I experienced one of the greatest surprises of my life. I had been visualizing how difficult it would be and how unhappy I would feel following Christ, when nearly all my associates were doing otherwise. But cost what it might, I had determined to go on with it. However, the moment I turned my life over to God, something happened that changed everything. My appraisal of values became different, my desires were purified and sublimated, and my whole outlook on life was changed. And to my great delight, a deep pervasive happiness and an all-inclusive peace possessed me (and have never left me from that day on) which transcended everything I had ever known, as far as real satisfaction is concerned.

Later on, I learned from the New Testament that such an experience is called a *new birth* in John 3:7, "Ye must be born again"; and the one having such an experience is called a *new creature* in 2 Cor. 5:17, "Wherefore if any man is in Christ he is a new creature: old things are passed away; behold, they are become new." But in 2 Peter 1:4, the reason for the change wrought is explained in these words, *partakers of the divine nature*. Or, in other words, because God has, on our invitation, come into our lives, He changes our dispositions, our attitudes, our desires and He motivates and directs us in keeping with His ever-right and perfect will.

During those days, the following words by Ella Wheeler Wilcox proved exceedingly helpful:

> One ship drives east and another drives west,
> With the self-same winds that blow.
> > 'Tis the set of the sails
> > And not the gales
> That tell them the way to go.
>
> Like the winds of the sea are the winds of fate,
> As we voyage along through life.
> > 'Tis the set of the soul
> > That decides its goal,
> And not the calm or the strife.

Furthermore, from that time onward, I had the benefit of God's guidance, and also His presence in overcoming temptation (1 Cor. 10:13), which the apostle Paul speaks of in Phil. 4:13 and 19 in these words. "I can do all things in Him that strengtheneth me . . . My God shall supply every need of yours according to His riches in glory in Christ Jesus."

That experience meant so much to me in improved character, personal happiness, and the feeling of security and abiding satisfaction, that I felt constrained to try to help others to have one like it. Not having completed grade school, I knew I must get a better education so I could command people's respect and to better persuade them. Accordingly, I asked my parents to release me from the lease on their ranch, so I could go to school. God prompted a Christian businessman to lend me as much money as I needed, until I graduated from college, ten years later. And

5

all through life God has opened one door after another and provided generously to meet every need.

Man's only hope for the highest type of self-realization here as well as hereafter is through accepting the Savior, who so loved us that He left Heaven and clothed Himself in flesh, shared the common lot of man, and even died an ignominious death on the cross that He might reconcile us to God. He has warned us of the futility and the hopelessness of human existence apart from Him in these words, ''For what doth it profit a man to gain the whole world, and lose his own soul?'' (Mark 8:36).

God's word declares what we already know through our consciences, that all of us are sinners and alienated from Him, ''All have sinned and come short of the glory of God,'' Rom. 3:23. And it also makes clear that no one in heaven or on earth, except one, the Lord Jesus Christ, is authorized to make peace between us and God, ''For there is one God, one mediator between God and men, the man Christ Jesus'' (Tim. 2:5).

Anyone can experience God's forgiveness and become a new creature. Both the question as to God's way of salvation and also the answer are found in Acts 16:30, 31. The Philippian jailer asked the apostles, Paul and Silas, ''Sirs, what must I do to be saved?'' And they responded, ''Believe on the Lord Jesus, and thou shalt be saved, thou and thy house.'' After the jailer did as they directed, which included confessing Christ by means of baptism, he ''rejoiced greatly, with all his house, having believed in God.'' The dying thief on the cross in his utter helplessness, with both his hands and feet nailed and unable to do anything to commend himself to Christ, prayed, ''Remember me when thou comest into Thy kingdom,'' he received this reply, ''Verily I say unto thee, today shalt thou be with Me in Paradise,'' (Luke 23:42, 43). And the publican received similar assurance, when he prayed ''God be thou merciful to me a sinner,'' for Jesus said of him, ''This man went down to his house justified,'' (Luke 18:13, 14).

The same Savior will respond in the same way to you, if you will sincerely turn your life over to Him. ''Him that cometh to Me, I will in no wise cast out" (John 6:37). "Verily, verily, I say unto you, He that heareth My word, and believeth Him that sent Me, hath eternal life, and cometh not into judgment, but hath passed out of death into life" (John 5:24).

Just as I am, without one plea
But that Thy blood was shed for me,
And that Thou bidd'st me come to Thee—
O Lamb of God, I come, I come.

Just as I am, and waiting not
To rid my soul of one dark blot.
To Thee, whose blood can cleanse each spot,
O Lamb of God, I come, I come.

Chapter 2

High Points in a Professor's Life

(The following article was written in 1960, the year of Dr. Mantey's retirement, but was not prepared for publication until April 1978.)

With the end of this school year, I shall have completed forty years of teaching; thirty-five in the Northern Baptist Theological Seminary in Chicago. In viewing that experience, there comes to mind some pertinent memories and convictions that may be worthy of sharing with others.

No doubt, all of us who are teaching seminary students realize how marvelously we are favored to have a part in training them, for they are people who have dedicated themselves to the noblest of all occupations. These are a special people who need to be blameless in character, well-balanced in personality, self-sacrificing in spirit, and disciplined and trained in mind. The level of civilization rises or falls largely according to the religious leadership that a generation has. We, then, have a vital part in determining what type of civilization will prevail during and following our generation.

To qualify for being the best type of biblical professor, one needs a genuine conversion experience, which to my mind, is an absolute prerequisite. The realization and assurance that we came to God with our burden of sin, asking for pardon, and that

8

the Holy Spirit assured us that we were forgiven and gave us peace and joy—that, and only that, is a basic foundation for adequate service in our profession.

Perhaps next in importance is the conviction that such an experience is so vital to everybody that, unless he has it, he passes into eternity without hope and without God. The urgency of man's need for God's pardon and favor grips and constrains us to try to help people make their peace with God by accepting the Savior whom he sent into the world. Like Isaiah, after his own sins were removed, we volunteer to communicate our faith and God's message, and say to God, "Here am I, send me!" So vital and essential has a right relationship with God become to us, that something of the compulsion that gripped the apostle Paul to say, "Woe unto me, if I preach not the Gospel," dominates our lives.

The Biblical Message Triumphs Over Its Critics

There have been various waves of theological thought during the last forty years, such as liberalism, fundamentalism, neoorthodoxy, evangelicalism, new evangelicalism, and other "isms," but one of the comforting satisfactions to me is that in spite of the fact that some young theologues are inclined to jump on each bandwagon of theological thought that is presented, like women following the new styles and fashions of dress, the trend of theological thinking, by people as a whole, is to swing back to accepting the Bible as authoritative in all matters of Christian faith and practice. Any deviation from that "general concept" is soon discovered to be inadequate. Critics of the right and the left attack any deviation and point out its shortcomings until it is found untenable. Then a new wave or fad of theological speculation makes its appearance and suffers a similar fate. The tendency, however, through all the centuries of Christendom, has been to accept the Bible as reliable historically, and as a supreme and dependable guide religiously.

The Gospel Is Relevant Today

I have observed that comparatively few open-minded people, have serious difficulty in accepting the teachings of the New Testament. In my forty years of teaching, I have been surprised to find that the vast majority of students found no serious intellectual handicap in believing the biblical message. It is sufficiently relevant to our modern culture to meet the needs of every man who sincerely seeks salvation with penitence and faith in Christ. Jeremiah's declaration is still true. "You shall seek me and you shall find me when you search for me with all your heart."

Unprecedented Crowds Attend Christian Services

The statement by a professor of sociology to the effect that nine-tenths of people are nonrational has a good deal of merit in it. Most people are not swayed by reason nearly so much as they are by emotions, social pressures, and other influences. Consequently, the enthusiastic proclamation of the Gospel as God's message for our time attracts and persuades people today, just as it did in the first century. People know they are sinners and that they need a Savior.

God's Love Versus His Wrath

God's limitless love and his punishment for sin were both exhibited in Christ's death on the cross. When Christ cried out in agony of body and spirit, "My God, my God, why have you forsaken me?" he revealed not only the bottomless depths of suffering for our sakes, but also the awfulness of the consequences of sin for unrepentant unbelievers. By his death, Christ opened and left open a door of free access to God's pardon, presence, and power.

However, although the New Testament speaks frequently of God's love, it also frequently mentions God's wrath. As biblical expositors, we are well aware of the fact that Christ himself taught that eternal punishment is to be the sad fate of the unsaved, saying, "They will go away into eternal punishment, but the righteous into eternal life" (Matt. 25:46), and he reiterated this harsh, difficult-to-believe doctrine, graphically and dramatically, in the portrayal of the rich man in Hades, who was informed that a vast, impassable gulf eternally separates the unsaved from the saved (Luke 16:26). What a tremendous incentive this should be to believers to persuade others to become Christians!

A First-Century Portrait of Christ

Have you ever imagined what kind of reception would be given a first-century portrait of Jesus Christ, which had been painted by an artist who knew him personally? How would the paintings of Christ by other artists in the following centuries compare in reliability and value with a newly recovered and well-preserved, *bona fide* picture of Christ? Would not the benefit of doubt favor the first-century painting, chiefly due to the fact the artist personally knew whom he was painting?

I'm so simpleminded and naive as to believe that we have such pen portraits of our Savior in the New Testament, and that whatever writers in succeeding centuries have written that differs from those accounts, can never compare in reliability and value with the first-century "originals." The further removed one is in time and in access from first-century sources, the less likely is he to contribute a better concept. To me, the first-century, eyewitness portraits are far more reliable than any that differ from them.

Incomparable Power in Christ

Dr. Amos N. Wilder, in his book, *New Testament Faith for Today*, pp. 5–7, has beautifully and forcefully portrayed in these words the tremendous significance of the revelation we have in Christ,

> Jesus' own life drama and the experience of His followers with Him and through Him released an incomparable power. This power was creative both in life and in thought. Here it was that the finger of God touched the world as though in a new day of creation. It was as though a spark had been struck between heaven and earth which gave the first community a new and blinding light on existence and which changed the face of the world. Jesus' career and teaching in that critical hour of Israel's history, offered the circumstance, but it was the whole drama and fate of Jesus, read in the light of the Scriptures, which set off the spark. . . . The ends of life were grasped with utmost clarity; the glory before, within and beyond the world was disclosed in glistening radiance. Our life in time was assigned immeasurable significance, since it was seen in its ultimate context.

The Incomparable Christ

Something happened here on earth in the life and teachings of Christ that was so marvelous and so significant that its appraisal transcends the comprehension of men. Unexpected and unimaginable moral and spiritual benefits were at that time released and made available to mankind. It is no wonder that the world now counts time by going back to his birth. God's eternal love, as perfectly portrayed in Christ, has drawn people ever since with its majestic and mystic charms. In at least six ways, he towers above all men of all time.

He Has Given Us Our Most Lofty Ideas of God

He so taught and lived that men have been asking ever since, "Is God as good as Jesus Christ?" He said of himself, "He that has seen me has seen the Father." God was portrayed as full of love and tender compassion toward all who turn to him with contrition and readiness to obey.

He Has Given Us Our Noblest Estimate of Man

Emerson has stated that Jesus alone rightly estimated the greatness of man. Jesus, unlike the leaders of his day, treated all, even the poor and outcasts, and enemies as well, with courtesy and respect.

He Has Given Us Our Highest Ethical Ideals

Through the centuries, his teachings stand out as peerless, timeless, transcendent, and incomparable. In simple words and loving deeds, he gave us a superlative standard of conduct. "Be ye perfect as your Father in heaven is perfect."

He Has Given Us Unlimited Resources of Spiritual Power

Nothing seemed too great for him to do. The sick became well, the lame walked, lepers were cleansed, and even the dead came to life at his command. He has made available through the Holy Spirit sufficient power to transform an unsocial, selfish, and sinful man into an unselfish and self-sacrificing citizen. As Paul said, "If any man is in Christ, he is a new creature. . . . I can do all things through Him who strengthens me."

He Has Given Us Our Greatest Example of Faith in God

Not only in His teachings did Jesus magnify the tremendous potentialities of faith in God, by such statements as, "If you have faith as a grain of mustard seed . . . nothing will be impossible to you" (Matt. 17:20); "All things are possible to him that believes" (Mark 9:21). Every day during his public ministry, he demonstrated triumphant faith.

He Has Given Us Our Best Manifestation of Love for Mankind

None ever loved as he did. Daily, during his adult life, he went about doing good. Here a mother is healed, there a son is restored to life, a brokenhearted Mary receives pardon and peace, a dead Lazarus is restored to life, and finally he offers up his life that all of us may have eternal life. No wonder his name is the most revered in all the world today.

Needed—Zeal for Christ

As a seminary professor, I'm inclined to believe that we reach our highest point of achievement and make our greatest contribution to our generation, not so much in the facts that we teach, nor in the books we write, as in the zest and zeal for Christ that we help to generate in the students we teach and in the people we contact. The apostle Paul's injunction that we, "Never flag in zeal; be aglow with the Spirit; serve the Lord" (Rom. 12:11) needs to be embodied in and manifested by religious educators, if they are to persuade and sway dynamically those that they teach. Information is plentiful in dictionaries, commentaries, in all kinds of books, and via radio and television, but truth, clothed in and mediated by dynamic, enthusiastic leaders, challenges and captivates people as nothing else can. Trained and experienced as we are in biblical studies, it behooves us to be exemplary in zeal as well as in knowledge.

Chapter 3

Christianity Versus Churchianity

Early in the second century A.D., there was a gradual drift away
from a few teachings in the New Testament. Dependence on
Christ alone for salvation, as a teaching, was modified by rules
on conduct and ritualism. In the third century, the drift was worse.
Pouring instead of immersion was practiced on dying people who
wanted baptism. However, if the person did not die, immersion
was insisted on. This was the approved form of baptism, even
up to the twelfth century. The teaching that baptism was necessary
in obtaining salvation led to infants being baptized, which was
not a custom in New Testament churches.

Besides, trust in Christ and willingness to obey him are
prerequisites to baptism and salvation. However, infants are
"blameless" and not lost. David said of a dead son, "I will go
to him." Jesus said to the repentant thief: "Today you will be
with me in Paradise."

The fact that Jesus was baptized in the Jordan River, and
the Ethiopian "went down into the water and Philip baptized
him," and "They both came up out of the water" (Acts 8:38–39)
implies that they got more than their feet wet.

John (3:36) wrote, "He who does not obey the Son shall
not see life, but the wrath of God rests upon him"; and Acts 2:38
reads, *"Repent* and be baptized *every one* of you in the name of

Jesus Christ for the forgiveness of your sins." So all Christians are commanded to be baptized, but *only after* they have repented!

In baptism one is joining those who have sworn allegiance to Christ and confessing him as Savior and Lord. It is a decidedly different crowd from the "world, the flesh and the devil." "Bad company corrupts good morals" (I Cor. 15:33). Good company (Christ) creates good morals!

The most radical and diabolical departure from New Testament teaching began about 220 A. D. Callistus (also known as Calixtus I) was a pastor in Rome and was the first, historically, to advocate and practice priestly absolution. Hippolytus stated about him *(Refutation of all Heresies,* Bx 1 × .7, in *Antenicean Fathers):* "The imposter was the *first* to invite making concessions to men's pleasures saying to all that sins were forgiven by him, and that the ark of Noah was made a symbol of the church, in which were dogs, ravens and all things clean and unclean. Or in other words, let those in the church who are guilty of sin remain in it."

Since Calistus was the *"first"* heretic to practice priestly absolution, that means that no apostle was guilty of doing so. Yet many claim Peter was authorized to do so in Matt. 16:18,19, and the apostles in Matt. 18:18. All Greek grammarians agree that the apostles taught the opposite of that. The correct translation of those verses is: "Whom do you say I am?" Simon Peter answering said, "You are the Christ the Son of the living God." Note this fact. Peter was declaring his belief, and the first to do so, that Jesus was the Messiah and the Son of God. Then Christ complimented him by saying: "Blessed are you *Simon son of John."* He did not call him Peter but he gave him an A-plus grade for believing and confessing that Jesus was the Christ and the Son of God, and said "You are a rock (petros), and upon such rocks (petra) I will build my church." (The word such is one of the meanings cited in *Arndt-Gingrich Greek Lexicon,* 602 [2 Tim. 3:5], "avoid *such* people.")

Petra was used as a collective noun in *Koine* Greek, meaning a large number of rocks, or cliff, most of the time, especially in the LXX *(Septuagint).* Liddell and Scott in their Greek lexicon have stated that *Petros* is a rock, usually a small one, and that the two words were never used interchangeably by good authors. *Petra* was frequently used also to mean a boulder and bedrock. Both God (Ps. 19:14; 62:02) and Christ were called *petra,* (1 Cor. 10:4), "The rock was the Christ."

Rock is the most durable substance for buildings. The Pyramids in Egypt and the Parthenon in Athens are examples.

Christ wants disciples who believe as Peter did and who are determined to do his will in spite of "hell and high water." Only such are to be members of his church. That is what Jesus told Nicodemus, "You must be born again" (John 3:7). Acts 3:38 declares the same fact. The reason why millions of people are not in churches is largely due to the fact that they have had sad experiences with members who have not repented and, therefore, are not born again, and so lack the presence and power of the Holy Spirit to motivate and strengthen them. He wants to do so and will do so when we determine to trust Christ and to *obey* him (John 3:36; Acts 2:38; 4:31; 5:32). It is deeply regrettable and actually damnable that some clergymen are not preaching and exhorting people that the church is not like Noah's Ark and that *only* regenerate people should belong to it.

Many people accept the heretical statement that "Peter was the foundation of the church," not knowing that statement has no biblical support. Instead, Eph. 2:20 informs us that all the apostles are called the foundation, of which the cornerstone, meaning basic foundation, is Christ and that all regenerate Christians are built on it also. In 1 Cor. 3:11, these words are found: *"For no other foundation can anyone lay* than that which is laid, which is *Jesus Christ."*

Chapter 4

The Perfect Tense and Paraphrastic Constructions

All group-translated Bibles, except the *American Standard Bible,* have mistranslations of John 20:23 and Matt. 16:19, 18:18 because the perfect tense is ignored. In the latest edition of the *American Standard Bible,* the publisher, The Lochman Foundation, fell from grace and reverted to the King James mistranslation, which is the opposite of what is in the Greek, Latin, and German; and, I have been informed, in five other languages, namely, in the Romanian, French, Italian, Spanish, and Esperanto. I know of no author of a Greek grammar who has advocated translating the perfect tense in John 20:23 as present. J. B. Rotherham, 1893; Father R. E. Knock, 1944; George Swann, 4th edition, 1947; C. B. Williams, 1952; Kenneth Wuest, 1961; and Alfred Marshall in *The Zondervan Parallel New Testament in Greek and English,* 1968, p. 55, have correctly translated that verse in their New Testaments.

An article by Morton S. Enslin, "The Perfect Tense in the Fourth Gospel," in JBL,LV, 124, supports that type of translation.

On page 111 of the Nestle *Interlineary Greek-English New Testament* is this sentence: "I am glad to see that Mr. Marshall has not missed the peculiar Greek construction in Matt. 16:19, what he 'binds on earth will be what has been bound in heaven.' "

The paraphrasis, *estai dedemenon,* in Matt. 16:19 and 18:18, in Greek grammars and in the Greek of the New Testament era meant "'shall have been bound,'" not "'shall be bound.'" The mistranslators apparently were not aware of that basic fact. Whenever the copula *einai* is used with a participle, if there are not words between them, there is a paraphrasis (also spelled periphrasis). To have the meaning "'shall be bound,'" the Greek words *estai demenon* are necessary. However, that participle is not in these passages. Instead of the present participle, there is the perfect participle *dedemenon,* meaning "'has been bound.'" The prefix *de* is on the perfect participle.

Since so many Bible translators have mistranslated the construction, I am citing statements from Greek grammarians on it.

C. F. D. Moule has been quoted as favoring the mistranslation in his *Idiom Book of New Testament Greek.* However, that is not a Greek grammar.

The *Blass-Debruner Greek Grammar,* Chicago University Press, translated by Robert W. Funk, p. 179, under the heading *Periphrastic Conjugations,* has nearly a whole page of discussion on the subject. Quote: "'The classical language had already made use of *einai* with the perfect participle as periphrasis for the perfect, pluperfect, and future perfect, active and passive. . . .it matters little whether one writes *epegegrapto* (A 17:13) or *ēn gegrammenon* (John 19:19f); *gegraptai* (very often) or *gegrammenon* (a) estin (John 6:31,20), and under "'examples of such usage"' Matt. 16:19; 18:18 are cited.

In *Goodwin's Syntax of Greek Modes and Tenses,* Macmillan, 1965, p. 13, quotation: "'The perfect represents an action as already finished at the present time or *gegrapha,* I have written, that is, my writing is now finished."' On page 14, "'The future perfect can be expressed by the perfect participle and *esomai* (the future form for *eimi*) which is exactly what is in Matt. 16:19 and 18:18, except that *estai,* the third person, future occurs instead of the first person, future.'"

Moulton, in his *A Grammar of the Greek New Testament,*

p. 88, has pointed out that in John 20:30–31, we have a paraphrasis in one verse and finite verb in the next with the same significance. "Which have not been written *(estin gegrammena)* in this book, but these have been written *(gegraptai)*."

William Douglas Chamberlain, author of *An Exegetical Greek Grammar,* Macmillan, has stated: "There are a few of periphrastics *estai dedemenon. . . .estai lelumenon* (Matt. 16:19). . . . They should be translated "shall have been bound" and "shall have been loosed."

Nigel Turner, coauthor with Moulton and Howard of *A Grammar of New Testament Greek;* and author of *Grammatical Insights into the New Testament,* Clark, Edinburg, p. 80, has written: "Whosoever sins you forgive, they have been forgiven (perfect). . . . Whatsoever thou bindest shall already have been permanently bound. . . . Matt. 16:19 and John 20:23 do not give a presbyter authority to decide which sins deserve forgiveness," p. 81.

A. T. Robertson, author of a 1200-page historical Greek grammar, has given us his interpretation of these verses in *Word Pictures in the New Testament* (V. 315). "The power to forgive sin belongs only to God. . . . There is no proof that he transferred to the apostles or their successors the power in and of themselves to forgive sins. In Matt. 16:19 and 18:18 we have a similar use of the rabbinical metaphor of binding and loosing *by* proclaiming and teaching."

Not only are Greek grammarians of this century unanimous on how to translate paraphrastic constructions, but so also were all translators of nonbiblical Greek literature. We learned that in a seminary group research study of thousands of pages of Hellenistic Greek authors. For example, "I feel that if I clear myself before you I shall have cleared *(apolelogemenos esesthai)* myself through you, before the rest of the Greeks" (Lucian, Philaris 1.1).

"Now if you do this, you will have bestowed *(ēsē katetetheiménos)* a great favor upon me" (Papyri, BGU 596.13). Other examples are in Lysias, XXII.19; XII,100; Papyri, Par. 14 and 50; 8.24.

21

Some individual translators of the New Testament who have correctly translated the verses under consideration are J. B. Rotherham, A. S. Worell, George Swann, A. Carr, C. B. Williams, Francis E. Siewert, Kenneth Wuest, J. B. Phillips, Gleason Ledyard; and B. W. Bacon of Yale in a translation of Matthew, and Randolph Yeager in *The Renaissance New Testament*.

Greek grammarians are specialists, experts on language construction and interpretation. If we do not accept their leadership, we will not preserve New Testament Christianity.

November 26, 1979

Editors of the Journal of Biblical Literature:

Should not the enclosed (my article on Paraphrastic constructions) appear as an article in JBL?

Fitzmyer once and Hayes twice have rejected articles of mine on this subject.

There seems to be a conspiracy to prevent people from knowing that only Christ can forgive sins against God. Cf 2 Cor. 5:18-19; John 14:6; Mark 2:7; and Luke 5:21.

In good exegesis all grammatical facts are explored.

I am asking you, the editorial board of JBL, to stop such biased, unscholarly, unbiblical, and anti-Christian discrimination.

Hopefully yours,
Julius R. Mantey

Chapter 5

Regrettable Mistranslations in the New Testament

Most, if not all, of the New Testament was first recorded in Greek. We have excellent translations of it, especially in our generation. However, there are still a few Greek words in it that are mistranslated.

One of these is in Revelation 3:14. The Greek word *archē* in most versions is mistranslated ''beginning,'' whereas it should be ''supervisor'' or another word with that connotation. ''The *supervisor* of God's creation.'' One of its meanings was ''first.'' In prepositional phrases—and there are many occurrences of it in the New Testament—it does mean ''beginning.'' But that word is misleading in Rev. 3:14. For instance, in Col. 1:16, it is stated that ''through him (Christ) every thing was created in heaven and earth.'' He was not created, or the beginning of the Creation. Rather, all through the New Testament, he is exalted as equal with God (Phil. 2:6; John 1:1).

Archē occurs in many Greek and English words as a prefix, denoting the leader or most outstanding person of those under consideration, namely, archbishop, archangel, or architect. In nonbiblical writers of the New Testament era, it was in frequent use, meaning the most outstanding leader, such as king, ruler, commander. In Philo, ''Amalek, the *king* of the nations.'' In

23

Plutarch, "He held the greatest and most exalted position as a *ruler.*" In the New Testament, it is so used depicting heavenly and earthly leaders. In Col. 1:18, "He is the head of the church, . . . the *preeminent one,* the first born . . . He alone should stand first in everything."

It is exceedingly strange that no translator, to my knowledge, has translated *archē* rightly in John 8:25. It is in a context where Jesus is affirming His deity and claiming to be the promised Messiah. Moses and other prophets had predicted that God would raise up another prophet whom people should follow. When Jesus was asked, "Who are you?" He simply answered, *"Tēn archēn,* the preeminent one,*"* i.e., the Messiah. The usual rendering of "beginning" is wrong.

By using the Greek word *houtōs* (so) as a conjunction instead of as an adverb in Rom. 11:26, many readers have misunderstood what the apostle Paul wrote. The word is derived from a pronoun meaning "this," and it never was used as a conjunction. Instead of the apostle Paul writing: "So all Israel will be saved," he wrote *"In this way* all Israel will be saved just as it is written" (Isa. 59:20). Repentance is specified as an absolute prerequisite to salvation (Acts 2:38).

In Matt. 1:18; 2:5, and 6:9 are excellent examples of the correct usage of *houtōs.* The fact that the Lord's prayer is introduced by it is significant.

Another misleading translation occurs in Heb. 12:2, "Who for, *(anti),* the joy that lay before him endured the cross." The word "for" in this verse is very inadequate. It does occur infrequently in passages where the meaning is "instead of," as Matt. 5:38, "An eye for an eye and a tooth for a tooth." But who would know that was the meaning it was to convey in the above verse? Rather, its most prevalent usage is in such sentences as: He was arrested for robbery (cause); He does this for fun (purpose); or He is gone for a month (duration of time).

By using one little word, *(anti),* "instead of," the author of Hebrews pictured the tremendous contrast in Jesus' life before and after his incarnation. Its dominant and prevalent meaning is "instead of" (Gen. 22:13; 44:33; Matt. 2:22; Luke 11:11).

24

Two words in Matt. 16:18, *petros* and *petra* are not translated adequately in most versions. To Jesus' question, "Who do people say the Son of Man is?" Peter replied, "You are the Christ the Son of the Living God." Since Peter had come to have the right understanding of Jesus, he was complimented with these words: "You are a rock *(petros)* and upon this type of *rock (petra)* I will build my church."

The authors of the most comprehensive Greek lexicon were Liddell and Scott. Their definition of these words is: *"Petros* a stone, piece of rock, and thus distinguished from *petra,* a ledge or shelf of rocks. There is no example. . .of *petra* with the significance of *petros."*

These words were *not* used interchangeably. The church is to have members with Peter-like faith. Origen, in the first extant commentary on Matthew, so interpreted Matt. 16:18: "For a *rock (petros)* is every disciple of Christ. . .and upon every such *rock (petros)* is built every word of the Church."

Another regrettable translation is that of Matt. 16:19, since most translators, until recently, have failed to translate the Greek perfect tense, which occurs twice in the verse. However, Professors W. F. Albright and C. S. Mann, in their commentary on Matthew, published by Doubleday Press, have given us this accurate rendering; "I will give you the keys of the Kingdom of heaven. Whatever you bind on earth will have been bound *(estai dedemehon)* in heaven, and whatever you release on earth will have been released *(estai lelumenon)* in heaven" . . . "The Latin Vulgate also translates as, "Will have been bound," "will have been loosed," exactly corresponding to the Greek.

For over 400 years, the Germans, through Martin Luther, have had such a translation as above. Why haven't we? Could it have been due to theological bias? For over 1600 years, it has been right in Latin.

Jesus did not say: "will be bound" but rather "will have been bound." Since J. B. Rotherham's version in 1893, twelve others have come off the press with correct translations of the future perfect passive in Matt. 16:19. This verbal construction

25

has always been translated properly in nonbiblical Greek. Only in the Bible is it mistranslated.

There is a similar oversight in John 20:23, where the word *apheōntai* occurs. Instead of the words "they are forgiven" we should have the following: "Receive the Holy Spirit. Forgive the sins of those who "have been forgiven" (by God). That is the translation in both Latin and German. Men are to ratify what God had decided or done. It is not the reverse. In the "summer" 1973 issue of *The Journal of Evangelical Theological Society* is an article of mine on the Greek perfect tense in the above verses. Another article on the same subject has been accepted for appearance in the *Review and Expositor* of the Southern Baptist Theological Seminary.

Genuine Christians who are indwelt by the Holy Spirit (Acts 5:32), have divine motivation that inhibits and restrains them from what is wrong and selfish. Not only this but they also are motivated to be kind and to practice love and helpfulness toward others. Isn't this mankind's greatest need? Such people are not contributing to the alarming increase of crime. Rather they have experienced a solution for it.

Chapter 6

Repentance and Conversion

The *Chicago Daily News* reported recently that Billy Graham, in talking about what Americans need most, stated: "It is absolutely impossible to change society and to reverse the moral trend unless we ourselves are changed from the inside out. Man needs transformation or conversion. . . . Our only way to moral reform is through repentance of our sins and a return to God."

The Old Testament in no uncertain terms reiterates the same truth over and over again. A representative and a very specific statement to that effect is found in 2 Chron. 7:14: "If my people, who are called by my name, shall humble themselves, and pray, and seek my face, and turn from their wicked ways; *then* will I hear from heaven and will forgive their sin and will heal their land."

The Meaning of Repentance and Conversion in the New Testament

Repentance. Two Greek words are so translated. *Metamelomai* has the basic connotation of feeling differently, or remorse (Matt. 21:29, 32; 27:3). Judas repented only in the sense of remorse, not with the idea of abandoning sin. Paul used this

27

word with such a meaning (2 Cor. 7:8). *Metanoia* (noun) is regularly used to express the requisite state of mind necessary for the forgiveness of sin. It means to think differently or to have a different attitude toward sin and God, etc.

Conversion. *Strepho* (*strophe,* noun), the root word, is used twice to denote conversion—Matt. 18:3: "Unless you become *converted* and become as little children you will not enter into the kingdom of heaven"; and John 12:40: ". . .become *converted,* and I will heal them." The prepositional prefix *epi* occurs on the word in the other passages where the sense of conversion is expressed. The basic idea of the word is to turn, and in most passages where it denotes conversion, it is used in the active voice.

The Usage of These Words in the New Testament

In two passages in the New Testament both of these words occur, and in both cases the word for repentance precedes the other. Acts 3:19: "Therefore *repent* and *turn* (be converted) in order that your sins may be blotted out, so that seasons of refreshing may come from the presence of the Lord"; Acts 26:20: ". . .that they should *repent* and *turn* to God and perform deeds worthy (i.e., expressive) of repentance."

In the above quotations we note that both words are used to describe an experience which has two aspects, namely that of turning away from displeasing God to pleasing him. And both words are used to denote the human volition and act by which man, convicted of sin by the Holy Spirit, determines to make his life conform to the will of God. Regeneration and justification are terms that denote God's part in transforming an individual, while the words faith, repentance, and conversion are used to express man's necessary response to Christ and God if regeneration is to be experienced.

Repentance without turning one's life over to God does not obtain remission of sins; neither does turning one's life over to God without repentance, as we shall indicate, being remission

28

of sins. Thus it is obvious that the two words deal with the right commitment of one's self to God with the definite intent of doing his will as long as life lasts. But before one makes such a life-transforming and epoch-making decision, he of necessity must have faith believing that God "rewards those who seek him" (Heb. 11:6). An example of this is cited in Acts 11:21, ". . .a great number that believed *turned* to the Lord."

The Emphasis Placed on Repentance in the New Testament

In Mark 1:4–5: "John the baptizer appeared in the wilderness, preaching a baptism of repentance" (i.e., a baptism expressive of repentance, genitive of description in Greek) "for the forgiveness of sins. And all the country of Judea and all the people of Jerusalem were going out to him, and, confessing their sins, they were being baptized in the river Jordan."
In Luke 3:7–14:

Who warned you, you serpent's brood, to escape from the wrath to come? See that you do something to show that your hearts are really changed [*metanoias*]! Don't start thinking that you can say to yourselves, "We are Abraham's children," for I tell you that God could produce children of Abraham out of these stones! The ax already lies at the root of the tree, and the tree that fails to produce good fruit is cut down and thrown into the fire.
Then the crowds would ask him, "Then what shall we do?" And his answer was, "The man who has two shirts must share with the man who has none, and the man who has food must do the same."
Some of the tax collectors also came to him to be baptized, and they asked him, "Master, what are we to do?" "You must not demand more than you are entitled to," he replied.
And the soldiers asked him, "And what are we to do?" "Don't bully people, don't bring false charges, and be content with your pay," he replied [J. B. Phillips's translation].

Matt. 3:5–12 is closely parallel to the statements in Mark and Luke, except that Luke has gone into greater detail in pointing out how the crowds, the tax collectors, and the soldiers were to demonstrate genuine repentance in their respective spheres of activity in society by using their time, talents, substance, and social position to serve others.

All three of the synoptic writers, we note, picture John the Baptist as being adamant in demanding real repentance and insisting on the expression of it in everyday living. They made it clear that being a descendant of Abraham was not enough, that fleshly descent would not abate God's wrath. Any Israelite who did not repent became subject to the severe judgment of God. But apparently, John also preached the necessity of openly and publicly confessing sins before or at the time of baptism, for both Mark and Matthew state that the baptismal candidates were confessing their sins. Furthermore, the repentance that was demanded was not to be only personal and negative, a cessation of sinning, but it was also to be social and positive.

However, we are indebted mostly to Luke for the detailed and specific spelling out of how one's repentance should and can be expressed in helpful acts of service to others. Jesus, like John, stressed the necessity of repentance and of true conversion. "By their fruits you shall know them. Not everyone who says to me, Lord, Lord, shall enter the kingdom of heaven, but he who does the will of my Father who is in heaven" (Matt. 7:20–21).

Repentance a Prerequisite to Baptism in the New Testament

Wherever any details are given, either by direct statement or by inference, repentance (also faith) was regarded as a necessary prerequisite to baptism, according to the New Testament record. In Acts 2:38, the priority of repentance to baptism is stated very definitely: "*Repent* and be baptized every one of you in the name of Jesus Christ for the forgiveness of your sins."

Certainly, it can be stated with less fear of contradiction that repentance was always regarded as a necessary prerequisite to forgiveness, as the above passage implies. Note also Luke 13:5; 24:47; Acts 8:22; 17:30.

The Philippian jailer demonstrated his repentance before being baptized by his washing and treating the wounds of Paul and Silas (Acts 16:33). Since baptism in apostolic times was a public confession of faith in Christ, it was very unlikely that anyone who had not repented and experienced regeneration would submit to baptism. For both among Jews and Gentiles, hostility to the point of severe persecution at times was experienced by new converts to Christianity. Social pressure was so intense against becoming a Christian that people would not have had the courage to break with family, community traditions, and customs unless the grace of God had been experienced in their lives. Repentance was a necessary prerequisite to that.

A correct interpretation of two expressions in the Greek New Testament throws additional light on this phase of the subject. One, *baptisma metanoias,* baptism of repentance, occurs four times, Mark 1:4; Luke 3:31; Acts 13:24, and 19:4. The word translated 'repentance' in this phrase is in the genitive case and is descriptive in function. It was a *repentance* baptism, i.e., the baptism was characterized by and expressive of repentance. Without question, the Lukan context in which the phrase occurs makes it very definite that baptism was not administered without some evidence of repentance. The Pharisees and Sadducees, the religious and political leaders at that time, who came to John for baptism, were called a ''brood of vipers'' and were told to ''bear fruits that befit *repentance''* (RSV, Luke 3:7–8). Or, in other words, John refused to baptize them on the grounds that they were not fit candidates for it. ''John demands proof from these men of the new life before he administers baptism to them'' (A. T. Robertsen in *Word Pictures in the New Testament,* vol. I, p. 8).

The other expression is in Matt. 3:11 and is translated in the RSV, ''I baptize you with (*in,* Greek) water for *repentance.''* The Greek preposition, translated *for* above, is *eis,* and is used to denote cause at times in the Greek of the first century and in the New Testament. Our word *for* can be used to express cause; for instance, "He was arrested for stealing." In at least four modern speech translations, *eis* is translated as having causal significance in Matt. 3:11. In Weymouth, it's *on profession of;* in Goodspeed, it's *in token of;* in Williams, it's *to picture;* and in Phillips, it's *as a sign of.* All of these are causal in force.

Since faith and repentance are New Testament prerequisites to baptism, how could an infant qualify for it?

The most exhaustive and recent scholarly discussion on the causal use of *eis* in Matt. 3:11 and in the Greek of New Testament times is found in the *Journal of Biblical Literature.* Four articles appeared on the subject, three in 1951 and in vol. LXX, and one in 1952, vol. LXXI. There were two by Ralph Marcus of the University of Chicago, and two by myself. Numerous examples from secular and sacred Greek were cited to illustrate and prove how *eis* was used with causal significance, one of which is taken from Gen. (in the LXX) 4:23: "I killed a man *for* wounding me, and a young man *for* striking me."

Repentance and Conversion in Everyday Life

As is generally known, people do not repent and become converted until they know that they are sinners and that they need the Savior. Hence, as a precursor to salvation, people of necessity must become informed of the salient elements of the Gospel. Until they realize that they are shortchanging themselves and are jeopardizing their future, that they have brought the eternal wrath of God upon themselves, there is little likelihood of their becoming converted and turning to Christ as Savior. Consequently, there is urgency that every means available should be used to proclaim and to live the Gospel, so as to lay the groundwork for the Holy Spirit to use the truth so disseminated to induce conviction and conversion. Jesus depicted graphically and bluntly the terrible doom that awaits the impenitent: "And they will go

32

away into eternal punishment, but the righteous into eternal life'' (Matt. 25:46).

Not only do men need to know that their sins will bring the inescapable judgment of God upon themselves, but also that they can never enjoy life in its fullness here and now until they have become converted and experience God's marvelous transforming grace. Jesus offered a better existence when he declared ''I came that they may have life and have it abundantly'' (John 10:10). He promised: ''that my joy may be in you, and that your joy may be full. . .and your sorrow will turn into joy. . .and no one will take your joy from you'' (John 15:11 and 16:21,22). The apostle Paul described this experience in these words: ''Wherefore if any one is in Christ he is a new creature; the old has passed away, behold it has become new'' (2 Cor. 5:17).

The only normal man is the converted man. Only then is he most free from the tensions and frustrations of life. He is most likely to be at peace, with both God and men. Then only does he enjoy in its fullness a clear conscience and freedom from guilt and fear. For the first time is he living in harmony with God's will for his life. The realization that God's favor is upon him and that ''all things will work together for his good'' cheers his spirit and fills his life with joyful expectancy. Like the Psalmist, he visualizes as his possession the ''goodness and mercy'' of God and expects to ''dwell in his house forever.''

Erik Routley, in *The Gift of Conversion,* describing the benefits of conversion, has stated: ''Personality is not blurred or made negative in conversion. On the contrary, the converted man is more a person than he was. The tension between what he is and what he would wish to appear to his neighbors is eased, and the result is a simpler, more direct, more clearly drawn personality. Confusion is replaced by integration and harmony.'' In Gal. 5:23, the apostle Paul has mentioned nine exceedingly precious acquisitions of life and character that become one's immediate or potential possession when he is truly converted: ''love, joy, peace, patience, kindness, goodness, faithfulness, gentleness, self-control.'' How lovely life would be if we and all whom we associate with always manifested such gracious characteristics!

Following is an illustration of the change that came into Eugenia Price's life immediately after her conversion: "I knew *Life* had found me! Glorious, sunfilled, Son-blended Life that would never let go. . . . This was a call back to the Natural. This was my Creator calling me into the Joy of Oneness with Him. This was 'from the beginning or ever the earth was' and this was new. This was a completely *new* life, just created in me. I had not learned to walk in it yet, but it was mine as Eternity was mine."

> Sinners, turn, why will you die?
> God, your Saviour, asks you—Why?
> He who did your souls retrieve,
> Died himself that you might live.
> Will you let him die in vain?
> Crucify your Lord again?
> Why, you ransomed sinners, why
> Will you slight his grace and die?
>
> —*John Wesley*

Chapter 7

Why Not Pray?

No Christian can live victoriously and fruitfully without prayer. Until prayer becomes vital and habitual, he fails to avail himself of God's presence, power, and plenty. He is without the divine resources that God has provided for him. He remains a spiritual weakling, neither triumphant in overcoming personal temptations nor fruitful in helping others morally and spiritually. "Watch and pray that ye enter not into temptation" (Matt. 26:41). "Apart from me ye can do nothing" (John 15:5).

> We kneel, how weak! we rise, how full of power!
> Why, therefore, should we do ourselves this wrong
> Or others—that we are not always strong—
> That we are sometimes overborne with care—
> That we should ever weak or heartless be,
> Anxious or troubled—when with us is prayer,
> And joy and strength and courage are with thee?
>
> *—Richard Trench*

Our Lord, although he was divine and sinless, nevertheless prayed frequently and fervently. Regularly, he asked God for guidance, wisdom, and strength. Before any significant event, he spent much time in prayer, ascertaining God's will and in receiving divine help. Thus, in example, as well as in numerous exhortations, he has taught us to pray regularly and expectantly. "Ask, and it shall be given you; seek, and you shall find; knock, and it shall be opened . . . . If you then, being evil, know how to give good gifts to your children, how much more shall your Father who is in heaven give good things to them that ask him?" (Matt. 7:7–11). Luke 11:13 has this same statement, except that he has substituted the words "Holy Spirit" for "good things." When the Holy Spirit indwells us, do we not also have the guarantee that good things will be forthcoming? For the presence of God is synonymous with the blessings of God.

Why Some Prayers Are Ineffective

God's Word specifies some attitudes and practices that are barriers to our receiving what we are asking for. One of these is selfishness. "You ask and do not receive, because you ask wrongly, to spend it on your pleasures" (James 4:3).

Another is a wrong attitude toward others. "If ye forgive men their trespasses, your heavenly Father will also forgive you" (Matt. 6:14). "Every one who is angry with his brother shall be in danger of the judgment" (Matt. 5:22).

Another is willfully harbored sin. In Ps. 66:18, we are told, "If I regard iniquity in my heart, the Lord will not hear me." On the other hand, James 5:16 says that "The prayer of a righteous man has great power in its effects."

Another is disobedience and unwillingness to do whatever God desires of us. "Beloved, if our hearts do not condemn us, we have confidence before God; and we receive from him whatever we ask, because we keep his commandments and do what pleases him" (1 John 3:22). If God is not Lord of all in our lives, he is not Lord at all. Willingness to do his will is therefore an absolute requirement for his favor.

My Jesus, as thou wilt!
Oh, may thy will be mine;
Into thy hand of love
I would my all resign;
Through sorrow, or through joy,
Conduct me as thine own,
And help me still to say,
My Lord, thy will be done!

—*Benjamin Schmolck*

Chapter 8

Christian Experience—An Incontrovertible Argument for Christianity

In trying to analyze my reasons for having made a special study of Christian experience, two things stand out in my mind. When I first became a Christian, I frequently heard slurring remarks made against Christianity in general and the authenticity of the Bible in particular. My conversion convinced me that the Bible was reliable, for it was from the reading of it that I received my impulse and the determination to commit my life to God for salvation and to ask him to save me. When I did that, I knew immediately that I had done the right thing, and was at peace, having full assurance that God had saved me. Ever since then, I have been anxious to defend Christianity on account of its unspeakable benefits to myself. I also feel that, because of the modern scientific attitude to give consideration to facts and especially because of the attitude of the philosophy of pragmatism, that whatever works is real and worthy of consideration, Christian experience is the best present-day defense for Christianity.

Dr. William James has given an inclusive definition of religious experience, (1) "An uneasiness, which reduced to its simplest terms is a sense that there is something wrong about us as we naturally stand. (2) Its solution, which is a sense that we are saved from the wrongness by making proper connection with the higher powers."

Dr. E. Y. Mullins gives the following definition: "Christian experience is the state or condition produced in the mental, moral and spiritual nature of man when he conforms to the conditions which Christianity declares to be necessary to union and fellowship with God." Christian experience includes all one's religious experiences, from conversion to death. Conversion is but the initial act of Christian experience.

Conversion may be analyzed as follows: (1) Repentance, which is a changed attitude toward sin and the abandonment of sin. It is the negative side of conversion. (2) Faith, which is an attitude of confidence in and submission to God. The object of faith is God in Christ. (3) The results of repentance and faith are intellectual peace and moral reinforcement. God's part in conversion or regeneration consists in imparting a new nature; in assuring the penitent that his sins are forgiven in furnishing him the continuous desire to stop what is wrong and to do what is right; in making the penitent peaceful and at rest in his inner being, with a consciousness that he has God's approval and God's goodwill; in reinforcing his will against sin; and in impelling him to render useful Christlike service to men.

Christian experience is primarily a relationship between two persons, God and man, as is effectively and forcefully illustrated in the publican's prayer, (Luke 18:13), "God, be thou merciful to me a sinner." "God" is on one hand and the "sinner" is on the other; "Thou" and "me." The publican directed his plea directly to God and God responded to the plea just as directly, for the record says that the sinner "went down to his house justified," which means that he and God were completely reconciled to one another. Matt. 11:29 gives invitation "Come unto me all ye that labor and are heavy laden and I will give you rest." This invites every burdened man to enter into a personal relation with Christ that he may have "rest" or peace.

There seems to be little data of religious experience in the personal sense, outside of Christianity. William James admits this in speaking of the lack of material other than Christian for

39

his study of religious experience. He says: "The absence of strictly personal confessions is the chief difficulty to the purely literary student who would like to become acquainted with the inwardness of religion other than the Christian."

In other religions, one is asked to accept certain statements about God and to govern his life thereby, in the hope of working out his own salvation. No conversion experience is thought of nor expected. No new nature is imparted, as in Christian experience. In Muhammadanism, salvation is obtained by carrying out a definitely stipulated program of deeds, such as repeating the Kalima, "There is no god but Allah, and Mohammed is his prophet"—saying prayers five times daily, giving alms, observing fasts, and visiting the city of Mecca. Their conception of God forbids a close personal relationship with him. Buddhism teaches that by observing the commands of the noble "Eightfold Path," one will finally become so exalted that he becomes a part of the divine essence and so loses his individual identity. Other religions are based on history that cannot be authenticated; they contain many gross, demoralizing, unprogressive teachings; and the religious experience of their adherents is confined merely to a knowledge of the supposed truths of those religions.

Christianity, however, has an authentic religious history, even back to God himself; its teachings are noble, uplifting, and progressive; and its religious experience does not consist merely of a knowledge about God, but of a personal, first-hand, intimate knowledge of God himself through fellowship with him.

In making a study of Christian experience, one does not need to go to a library to search historical documents, for he can find Christian experience in all of its varieties and forms in present-day Christians. It is the living miracle, still extant, being multiplied by millions in each generation. A large percentage of our nation's population can testify to the reality of Christian experience. One needs but to question and observe his neighbors to make a scientific study of Christian experience these days.

The testimony from witnesses who have had personal experience with an object is the best testimony obtainable, according to our court procedure. Only a few witnesses are considered sufficient to establish the evidence in question in a court, but Christianity has "so many" witnesses that they number into the hundreds of millions, who are unanimous in their testimony as to the reality of their Christian experience and the value of Christianity to themselves. If we glance toward the past, we can discover that the experiences of Christians in every succeeding generation from the Resurrection until now, bear witness to Christ's power to redeem men of every country, every race, and every generation who trust in Him for redemption. Every new generation has learned the Christian Gospel from living and original witnesses to the power and grace of the living Christ and has then transmitted the truth, confirmed and authenticated by its own experience, to the next generation.

These witnesses have been and are from every rank and file and station of life. They are of every occupation and profession. They are of every age from the years of accountability to the last moment of life. They are representative men of every degree of intelligence, from the man of little knowledge up to the intellectual giant. The simple man and the profound man both have a common religious experience and testify to its reality.

Furthermore, the character of Christianity's witnesses is reliable and authoritative. The men most trusted and reliable in our national and business life are Christian men. This fact alone should be enough to favorably dispose any man toward the validity of Christian experience. Because of so many witnesses, and with witnesses of the most reliable type to affirm their faith in Christianity, due to personal experience with Christ, Christianity has multiplied, unimpeachably, and authoritatively, with compelling evidence.

The fact that Christianity produces a wholesome change and often a striking, conspicuous change in the man who accepts it is an undeniable argument. The apostle Paul had a complete revolution of purpose in his Damascus road experience. Prior to that day, his whole tendency was against Christ and his believers; after that day, his whole tendency was toward Christ and his believers. Before, he was seeking to destroy Christianity; after that experience, he was seeking to build up Christianity. Although

41

the change may not be so marked in every believer, yet there is always a change in motive and tendency produced in conversion. The outward evidence of conversion is manifested by a crisis and a change in life. The change is visible to all the acquaintances of believers. To attribute the change to something else besides religion is not a valid objection. What is in consciousness is that the religious state and the change are related as cause and effect. Dr. George A. Barrow, author of *The Validity of Religious Experience,* says, "The consciousness of something that is able to affect and change man's life." City missions operated by men who had fallen into evil and despair and who attribute their transformation to religion is an everyday proof to its reality. If we admit that the normal man's mind is reliable, we must accept the unanimous testimony of converted men that the change is effected in connection with religion.

The following two testimonies are given as examples of Christian experience, having occurred within a half century of one another.

John Tyler, who was a descendant of President Tyler, was reared in a good home and was a college graduate. Flush with money, he became a globetrotter, a moral debauch, a hopeless, helpless drunkard and a prisoner in many prisons. Poverty finally claimed him, and he peddled cheese on the streets of New York, pawning his overcoat often, to get enough capital with which to begin anew. Since the earnings of the former day had been spent in drink and debauchery the preceding night with no hope of being able to reform and with broken health, he left a foreign land to come to his homeland to die. He was sitting in a park in New York one day, when a man came to him and suggested that he try God. He realized that he had tried everything else he knew of to break his bad habit and all to no avail. That night, he heard Jerry McAuley tell how low and helpless he had been and how God had saved him. McAuley's Christian experience gave Tyler hope that God would also help him, so he prayed to God that night in the mission. Immediately, peace and power and happiness came into his life. In his own words, he became a rejuvenated man, changed from a beast with swollen feet and body, to a man blessed with sweet repose, elastic step, bouyant spirit, steellike muscles, and bubbling over with love for the Christ who was the only power that could render inoperative his old habits and break the chain that for thirty years had kept him in slavish captivity.

Cliff Van Note, of whom I have come into recent acquaintance while participating in a panel discussion on "doctrine," related this experience to me.

On October 29, 1950, while on a mission involving the direction of fighter and bomber strikes in Korea, my plane was shot down approximately twenty-two miles behind the enemy line. While going down, the cloud cover completely kept from view the ground and the mountains, and made it impossible for both the pilot and myself to jump by parachute. We simply crashed abruptly in the side of a mountain. While going down, suddenly, the clouds opened and the green leaves of the trees could be seen with a clarity induced by fright. I yelled out "Lord save me," asking of course for Him to save my flesh from impending death. He did. Both the pilot and I survived. Our plane was the seventh plane of the original seven AT-6's in Korea to get shot down and we were the first two to live. My head was bleeding profusely from a wound received before the crash, but miraculously, except for minor bruises and abrasions, we were both in good condition when the North Koreans captured us. I noticed my head beginning to ache with varying degrees of severity which lasted continuously over the next nine-year period until my "confrontation" with Jesus Christ.

In 1956, my wife had received Jesus Christ in a tent meeting in Blytheville, Arkansas, where a young boy had been preaching. She had a definite transformation, with an added sweetness and patience toward me which was genuine and not "put-on." She witnessed to me of her experience and I with little respect agreed that it was a nice thing for her, and then continued my own life with renewed vigor undergirded with alcohol. I noticed her life was consistently good and with patience. I used alcohol in vain attempts to alleviate the pain in my head that I was never without. I tried many ways to see if I could destroy her faith, but I could not. Her life had become a life of "praise and glory to Jesus Christ." Then in November 1959, while lying out on a bed in East Orange, New Jersey, unable to move my arms and legs and little ability to speak, my wife entered the bedroom, looking with pity upon me, and asked if I wanted the doctor or the preacher. I couldn't verbally respond, and she called for a preacher who lost no time in getting to my bedside. He told me of the work of Jesus Christ. He didn't speak to me of my pitiful condition, he spoke only of the work of Jesus which was done in my behalf through His love for me. I thought to myself what a wonderment, that God would die for me, who was so miserable in the pain of sin and the pain of sinful flesh. The words that that preacher spoke to me touched my heart. He told me that the Holy Spirit was at that moment drawing me to the point of decision, and that I was now responsible before the God who became incarnated in flesh, who died willingly in my place for the penalty of sin which I should have paid, but that He substituted His life for mine willingly through His love. Oh how I wanted to shout out to Jesus, but I was physically unable. Instead, I prayed with this visiting Assembly of God preacher, in my mind, and gloriously felt the weight of sins forgiven lifted from my life. I breathed easier, and within a couple of days, the paralysis had left me as it had on so many other occasions, but the pain in my head remained.

The Friday night following, I was to attend my first church service. It was a Friday night prayer meeting. We picked up a young married woman, along with my two children and proceeded down busy Main Street of East Orange. The pain in my head continued to a severe extent and I knew that before we would reach our destination, I would again lose control of my neck muscles, and my eyes were becoming hazy. I cried out to the Lord not to let me lose my sight, and at that moment my wife reached over to hold my head in an upright position. With this help I reached the small church, which was next to the Roman church. When I stopped the car, my wife opened

44

her Bible to James 5:13–16. I read it and was amazed. I grabbed her Bible and ran inside the church, not paying any attention to the thirty or so persons who were praying together. I called out "Who are the elders?" The preacher who had visited me at home came to me along with a couple of deacons. I pointed out to them James 5:13–16, and with finger pointed to the very words, I demanded that they lay hands on me and pray for me as the Word instructed and that I would then get well. With looks of astonishment, they laid hands on me and independently prayed for me. About this time my wife, the young married woman, and my children entered. My feet felt as though they supported no weight; I felt physically as though I would lose my balance. With this feeling I realized that my nine-and-a-half-year headache had disappeared. My joy was uncontrollable; it was openly uninhibited. I praised my Lord for what I believe He did for me.

The following Sunday, I was to hear my first preaching service. He preached on John 3:16. Upon hearing the challenge of the closing prayer, I hurriedly left the church in advance of everyone, including my family,.and upon going outside saw a couple leaving the Roman Catholic church next door. When they reached the outer sidewalk, I rushed to greet them. They stopped, not knowing for sure what I was about to do or say, and then I told them of the wonderful thing that Jesus Christ did for me. I had memorized John 3:16, and repeated it to them. I knew no other verse, but the preacher said God's Word would not go void, and I believed him. I repeated it again and invited them to pray with me on the sidewalk in front of the two churches. They did. From that moment those two, who in like faith believed Jesus Christ for salvation, began to attend the church next door which spoke the message of a "Living Savior," Who lives and reigns in our hearts. I knew I was born again, not because of the "sign" of healing, but because of His Word which was proven true to my very own heart. He lives and now I know that I live.

Even though a grandfather, Brother Van Note feels the call

45

of God in his life and has just completed degree work at Luther Rice Seminary. He has been selected to rewrite many of the courses within the "master's program," and will go on with the ultimate goal of doctor of theology. He is still a soul-winner and leads many, including the major cultists, to a saving knowledge of Jesus Christ.

Chapter 9

The Psychology of Conversion

This happened in November 1915, in the small town of Sturgeon, Missouri. His name was Mat Hicks, and he was known as the vilest curser in the town as well as a drunkard. A few weeks before, he had been locked up in the town jail as a protection for his wife and children, for he had been found beating his wife while drunk. He was forty-eight years old. It was the second time he had gone to a preaching service in ten years, excepting now and then to a funeral. What prompted him to go to church these times? There is a touch of divine pathos in that intimate piece of information. This rough man, with such stern and uninviting appearance, and with such a loud, rasping voice, whose outward appearance would lead one to infer that his finer sensibilities had been smothered and strangled, was at heart fatherly and wanted his children to attain to the best. It was a spark of nobility of soul, which when properly quickened, inflamed his whole being with the desire and purpose to become a better father.

His boy, who was about six years old, was sitting on his knee and with childlike curiosity asked the father what happens to people when they die, and how he might make sure of gaining admittance into heaven. The father tried to answer these questions to his son's satisfaction, but in answering them, he became conscious that he was not setting the proper example before his family and that he was a hindrance to their getting to heaven. He realized with tremendous forcefulness that he was not the right kind of father and husband.

It was this serious thinking about his sinfulness and unworthiness that impelled him to go to church. The second time he came out, I noticed that he listened with exceptional attentiveness. After the benediction, he seemed to hesitate about leaving the church. At any rate, after I had shaken hands with him and noticed that he seemed responsive, I asked him if he would mind if I walked part way home with him. He seemed pleased. On the way home, I urged him earnestly to become a Christian. He then told me with deep anxiety that when he was a young man, he had tried to become a Christian, but had never experienced any change and that he doubted whether he could ever be saved. I assured him that if he would determine to do God's will and ask God to forgive and save him, I knew he could be saved there and then, and I asked him if he was willing to do that. To my delight, he said that he was.

Well, a cold November wind was blowing, and when I suggested that we pray, he suggested that we do so in the house. We stepped in. The wife and children were all in bed. There were no rugs on the floor, there was no fire, and the chairs and other furniture would scarcely hold together—they were so dilapidated. In a word, I explained to the wife, who happened to be a Christian, my purpose in being there. We knelt immediately beside rickety chairs for prayer. I prayed, and then I asked him to pray. That was the most thrilling prayer I had ever heard. It was as sincere and genuine as God's sunlight. With his whole body heaving with great sobs and with deep solemn pathos in his voice, he asked God to make him a better father and a better husband. He promised God that if He would save him, he would do all he possibly could to please him. He hadn't any more than gotten that thought expressed when he arose with his whole body quivering and his face aglow, and he grabbed my hand and announced with all the delight his voice could convey, "Brother, I've got it," meaning that the experience of salvation or conversion that he had once sought was now his actual and conscious possession. Being a young minister, who had witnessed but few conversions, I too was thoroughly happy. I stayed there for an hour or longer, listening to that man relate reminiscently how his mother had been grieved over his waywardness, and how on this occasion he felt inclined to turn, and how on that he had again resisted the tide of influences that prompted him to become a Christian.

On my next preaching trip to that place three weeks later, I called to see him. Then he told me with triumph and deep joy how even though he worked with section hands on the railroad, who were all rough and unconverted men, and who ridiculed him for claiming conversion, for the first time in years he had kept from cursing and that he was no longer bothered with the appetite for drink; and he made this meaningful remark, "The happiest three weeks of my life have been the last three weeks." It was hard for his neighbors to believe that such a coarsened sinner could be genuinely converted. His consistent and aggressive Christian living gradually convinced even the most skeptical. The last time I saw him, he told with joy how he helped two hardened sinners like he had been to trust Christ. The realization that I helped that man find Christ and peace when he seemed so far away from those transcendent blessings is one of the brightest and most delightful remembrances I possess.

James has defined conversion as, "the process, gradual or sudden, by which a self hitherto divided, and consciously wrong, inferior and unhappy, becomes unified and consciously right, superior and happy in consequence of its former hold upon religious realities." The word, in its Latin derivation, means turning, i.e., turning from one state or thing to another. In its broad sense, there are numerous conversions in every man's life, especially in the life of a man of character. In Christianity, however, it means to turn from living in sin and for self, to living in righteousness and for God and others. It deals only with the human side of regeneration. There can be almost as many types of conversions as there are conversions. The form the experience takes depends largely on the temperament of the individual. Peo-

49

ple of an intellectual type usually have a quiet, deliberate conversion, while those of an emotional type the opposite.

From a psychological basis, conversion begins in the subconsciousness. Some thought entering the mind starts an association of thoughts, which brings together past experiences, training, or ideals that produce, as James says, "a sense of uneasiness." How important then that the mind from earliest childhood be stored with such ideas and memories as will some day be the treasures that will be brought out to enrich the whole destiny of the personality.

In my own case, when I was sixteen years old, a boyhood sweetheart's explanation as to why she could not afford to go with me any longer—was—"On account of your conduct." This penetrated the deepest recesses of my mind. I asked myself if it had come to that, that a decent girl could not afford to associate with me any longer. It was such self-condemning thoughts that prompted me to begin reading the Bible, the way having been pointed out therein to a higher life—I decided to do God's will and trust him to save me. After I had become convinced that I was a sinner and was displeasing in the sight of some people, as well as God, my emotions impelled me to act—which is a second stage in conversion. The third stage is the determination or volition to live the Christian life. Expressing it in theological terms, it is conviction of sin—a sense of sin in one's life and a dissatisfaction because of it; next, it is repentance or turning away from sin—changing the mind about it; then it is faith—the positive committal of the soul to God, trusting him for forgiveness and for continued goodwill, with a readiness to please and serve Him, i.e., to be obedient.

As a teacher of Greek, it has been very illuminating to me to discover from independent researches in Xenophon and in the *Septuagint* that *"pistis,"* πιστις, "faith," had as a regular meaning in those writing, the idea of "loyalty" and "faithfulness." More than half of the time in the LXX, it has that meaning and it means that twice in Xenophon's *Anabasis*. As a confirmation of this, it is translated rightly in Titus 2:10, "not purloining, but showing all good fidelity." It is also properly translated 'faith-

50

fulness' in Gal. 5:22. The reason I mention this is to emphasize the fact that to exercise faith toward God, when one takes the meaning of the Greek word into consideration, means to not only believe in Him and to trust Him, but also to be faithful to Him, which implies obedience from the viewpoint of deliberate and voluntary submission. The opposite of *"pistis"* πιστις is *"apistia,"* απιστια which is translated, even in the New Testament, as disobedience, at times. Another sidelight on this interesting phase of conversion is the meaning of the word *"apeitheo,"* απειτεω which in the Revised Version, in John 3:36, is properly translated 'disobey'—"The wrath of God abides on those that disobey Him.'' From my studies of it in the LXX, classical Greek, the papyri, and the New Testament, it means regularly 'to disobey.' Then the word *"akouo"* ακομω points in the same direction that *"pistis"* πιστις does. One of its regular meanings, as well as "to hear," is "to heed" or "to obey." Thus, we can translate, "He that obeyeth my words and believeth on Him that sent me hath eternal life," or "My sheep heed (or obey) my voice and they follow me.''

One of the most practical suggestions we learn from psychology with reference to conversion is the fact that the processes of conversion begin in the subconscious mind. That being true, the wise and diplomatic thing to do is to make such an appeal, either in private or public, as will call forth out of the subconscious into the conscious such associations of thought as will create enough emotional stimulus to prompt the will to act favorably on the suggestion to become a Christian. One of the most effective appeals has always been to call up the tender, sacred memories concerning mother and her ideals for her child. That helps one to realize his sinfulness, as he contrasts himself with his mother and her faith in and devotion to God.

Another effective way is to point out to people the values of the life they are denying themselves in not being Christians. Such practical benefits as pardon, peace, love, hope, and assurance that one has God's forgiveness and divine favor, as well as having an eternal home in the Utopia of eternity, are gleams of light that penetrate many sordid and beclouded souls and pointing out the way to greater peace and satisfaction. Along this line, J. H. Snowden, in his *The Psychology of Conversion,* has forcibly stated this fact in a few words. "The way to move the will to obedience is to stir up the appropriate feelings, and the way to stir the feelings is to create and intensify the proper thought, and the way to create the thought is to present some efficient object that operates by the explosive power of a new interest."

Chapter 10

New Testament Backgrounds

Alexander the Great began the Greek invasion of the Near East in 334 B.C.; that same year, he defeated the Persian army at Granicus in Asia Minor, and again the following year at Issus. In 332 B.C., he reached the Phoenician coast (Lebanon) and captured Sidon and Tyre after a long siege. Proceeding south, he was welcomed in Jerusalem without resistance and with regal reception. The Jewish priests were in ceremonial costumes and the citizens were dressed in white garments (Josephus, *Antiquities,* Book XI, VIII, 5). This friendly demonstration influenced Alexander to offer the Jews generous terms. No one was taken into slavery, they were permitted free enjoyment of their laws and religious liberties, and they were exempted in sabbatical years from paying taxes. Thousands of young Jews enlisted in Alexander's army and marched south to help him conquer Egypt, then helping to subdue what remained of the Persian army in the Near East.

Seventy cities were colonized and settled by people friendly to Alexander and became centers of Greek culture, including Antioch, Jerusalem, and Alexandria. Greek sports became so popular that Jewish priests were accused of neglecting duties to participate in them. Greek philosophy and culture were generally received and entered into dynamic competition with Jewish concepts and culture. Polytheism, especially, became a snare to the Jews. But when Antiochus Epiphanes, a Syrian ruler, sought to force polytheism upon the Jews, the Maccabean revolt ensued in 167 B.C. After twenty-five years of guerrilla wars, bloody struggles, and costly sacrifices, the Jews won independence, first religious and then political, and they maintained it until 63 B.C. Then the Romans marched in and took over.

Benefits Derived From the Greeks

An outstanding and providential benefit of Greek culture to the Jews was the Greek language. For three and one-third centuries prior to Christ's birth, the Jews had been exposed to it. Since it was advantageous to them to learn to speak and to read Greek, they became a bilingual people.

Ptolemy Philadelphus, who became king over Egypt in 283 B.C., is credited with having invited the Jews to send able scholars to Alexandria in Egypt to translate the Hebrew Old Testament into Greek (Josephus, *Antiquities,* XII, 2). This translation is called the Septuagint and is abbreviated LXX, meaning seventy. Well-received and widely read, this translation became a notable factor in popularizing the use of Greek in services of worship and in furnishing a religious vocabulary for Christians. Most of the quotations in the New Testament come from the Septuagint.

Of all ancient languages, the Greek language was the best medium for accuracy of expression. In New Testament times, it was better in this respect than it is now. It had eight cases which, with the use of prepositions, facilitated stating truth unambiguously. Its tense system exceeded that of all the other ancient languages in making unmistakably clear what a writer had in mind. In addition to the tenses that we have in English, the Greeks had an *aorist* tense, the chief function of which was to state the single occurrence of an act or event, whereas the *present* tense was used to express continuous or repeated action. The fact that the *aorist* tense occurs in 1 John 2:1 in the verb "sin" makes clear that John was urging Christians to abstain from all sin:

"These things I write unto you that you not sin at all." However, in 1 John 3:9, where the verb "sin" occurs in the *present* tense, the correct translation is, "He that is born of God does not continue sinning." The use of the Greek *present* tense in 1 John 3:8 makes clear that to the apostle John, habitual indulgence in sin was proof that one was not a Christian: "He that continues practicing sin is of the devil."

Not only through its complex and adequate verb system, but also because of its extensive philosophical, ethical, and religious vocabulary, the Greek language was the best vehicle for the record of God's glorious revelation in Christ given in the New Testament. Modern Romance languages, as well as the English language, have deep roots in Greek. So much of the Greek has been assimilated into the English, that of the approximately five thousand words in the Greek New Testament, about one-fifth of them have been transliterated into the English language, as a whole or in part. Many times, only a syllable, such as a prefix or a suffix, has passed into the language, but frequently whole words from the Greek have become a part of our English vocabulary: paradox, paradise, planet, plastic, plethora, pleurisy, pneumatic, pneumonia, poem, police, polygamy, polyglot, polygon, and many others.

The Jews Under Roman Domination

When the Roman general, Pompey, invaded Judea and captured Jerusalem in 63 B.C., Jewish independence came to an end. Like Alexander the Great, Pompey followed the Roman governmental custom of not interfering with religious customs. He permitted Hyrcanus, the high priest, to exercise full liberty in matters of worship. Pompey started back to Rome soon afterward with the Jewish king, Aristobulus, his wife, and four children, in order to have them as a part of his exhibit of conquered rulers and their families for his triumphal procession in the city of Rome.

To understand what follows, we need to go back in history. In 129 B.C., the Idumeans, descendants of Esau, who lived between Judea and Egypt, were conquered by the Jews and given a choice: either leave their country empty-handed, or accept the Jewish religion, outwardly at least, by submitting to circumcision. They chose the latter.

Herod the Great was an Idumean. Although not a real Jew at heart, he became king of the Jews. Herod's father, Antipater, had become a general in the Jewish army. Not many years after the Romans invaded Palestine, they appointed Antipater as chief civil ruler over the Jews. He appointed his son Herod over the territory of Galilee, where Herod distinguished himself and won favor from the Romans. Herod was a very astute politician and a man of forceful character. He managed time after time to ingratiate himself with those over him in government. With high taxes collected from the Jews, he bribed governors and emperors, and so gained political favor that in 42 B.C. he was appointed tetrarch of Judea. In 40 B.C., when soliciting help in Rome after the Parthians had invaded Judea, he was given the title of king by the Roman senate, and was subsequently aided by a Roman army in driving out the Parthians.

The Parthians had helped Antigonus, a son of Aristobulus, deposed by Pompey in 63 B.C., to become king of Judea. The Jews preferred Antigonus to Herod, since Antigonus was a descendant of the famous Maccabean kings. So they had sided with the Parthians in fighting against Herod and the Romans. But Herod, the unwanted Idumean, regained dominion and was reinstated as ruler in 37 B.C.

Herod took immediate steps to destroy more than 100 outstanding Jewish citizens, including all but two members of the Sanhedrin, on the ground that they had supported Antigonus.

Herod had at least ten wives. Most favored of these was the beautiful Mariamne, who was of royal Jewish descent. But Herod's sister, Salome, was jealous of her and, by insidious innuendo and slander, created suspicion in Herod's mind as to Mariamne's loyalty.

Owing to pressure from the Jews, Herod appointed Aristobulus, brother of his wife Mariamne, as high priest. So popular was this appointment that Herod feared for his own position and had his brother-in-law drowned. Within a few years, Herod had executed one relative of his after another. Some of these were his mother-in-law, Alexandra, and her father, Hyrcanus, a high priest; his uncle, Joseph; and his favorite wife, Mariamne. In 6 B.C., he had two of his sons executed, Alexander and Aristobulus, sons of Mariamne.

It was within a few months of this time that Herod sent out the brutal order to slay all the children in Bethlehem two years old and under, since he had learned from the wise men that a child destined to become king had been born there.

At the age of seventy, a few days before his death in 4 B.C., on the ground that his son Antipater had plotted to succeed him in office, Herod had him killed. Herod's will specified that three of his sons should reign over his dominion: Archelaus over Judea and Samaria; Antipas over Galilee and Perea; Herod Philip over Auranitis, Trachonitis, and Batanea, which were situated north and east of Lake Galilee. Fearing that people would not mourn when he died, Herod gave orders to arrest hundreds of eminent Jews and to have them slain on the same day that he died. However, after his death, the members of his family refused to acquiesce in such brutality.

Archelaus was unpopular as a ruler from the very beginning. A delegation was sent to Rome to protest against his confirmation as ruler by the emperor Augustus, but their mission failed. His rule was full of injustice, gross cruelty, and wanton slaughter of Jewish citizens. He was unable to establish and maintain order. Consequently, in A.D. 6, he was deposed and banished to Gaul, and his property was confiscated.

He was succeeded by Coponius, a Roman, who had the title of procurator. Several Romans served in this capacity between A.D. 6 and 26, when Pontius Pilate was appointed. On one occasion, Pilate took temple funds (*corban,* Mark 7:11) to pay for an aqueduct that channeled water into Jerusalem. When thousands of Jews demanded the return of these funds, Pilate had a large number of them wounded and killed (Luke 13:1). Pilate met with growing opposition and was deposed after ten years in office.

Such acts of misrule alienated the Jews more and more and

tended to bring on the revolt of A.D. 66 that lasted four years and culminated in the destruction of the temple and Jerusalem in A.D. 70.

New Light From the Dead Sea Scrolls

While the Dead Sea Scrolls, some of which were first discovered in 1947, throw light mostly on Old Testament books, they nevertheless contribute considerably to a better understanding of the New Testament. They give us a vivid picture of the religious and cultural customs that were prevalent when John the Baptist and Jesus of Nazareth challenged their contemporaries. Many affinities of thought and language are common to both the New Testament and the scrolls. Such terms as "the elect," "light and darkness," "sons of light," "the two ways," "lake (river) of fire," occur in both. There are both similarities and differences in ideas and practice. Both held that the rite of induction into the order by immersion in water had no saving benefits. Communal fellowship was compulsory among the Covenanters (Essenes), but optional with the Christians (Acts 4:32–37).

Whether John the Baptist was influenced by the Essenes is doubtful, but there is no question about his agreement with them on the necessity of genuine repentance as a prerequisite to baptism (Luke 3:7–17). Josephus (*Antiquities,* Book XVIII, 5.2) confirms the emphasis on the need of repentance before baptism: "John commanded the Jews to exercise virtue both as to righteousness towards one another and piety toward God and so to come to baptism; that baptism would be acceptable to him, if they made use of it, *not in order to the putting away of some sins,* but for the purification of the body; supposing that *the soul was thoroughly purified beforehand by righteousness''* (italics mine). Translators of the New Testament into modern speech, such as Weymouth, Goodspeed, and Williams, therefore render Matt. 3:11 in this way, "I indeed baptize you in water because of repentance.''

58

How the New Testament Canon Developed

After the ascension of Christ, as churches were formed and Christianity expanded, no New Testament books existed as authoritative sources for preaching the Gospel. The Old Testament was regarded as inspired both by Jews and Christians, and parts of it were read regularly and expounded in synagogue and church worship services. Christians made effective use of messianic passages to show Jesus of Nazareth as fulfillment of them.

Believers were dependent upon the testimony of people who knew and had heard what the Savior said and did. Hence, the witness of the apostles became the chief authoritative source for establishing and confirming the reliability of all information pertaining to Christ.

While the apostles were alive and their testimony was available, and the preaching of the Gospel was limited to Palestine and contiguous areas, the need for written records was not urgent. However, after the death of the apostles, and others who had seen and heard the Lord Jesus, the situation changed. If the events of our Savior's life and his teachings had not been written, we would be dependent merely upon hearsay and tradition.

Fortunately, through God's providence and the impulsion of the Holy Spirit, some of the apostles and other intimate associates who saw and heard them frequently, have given us written, authoritative, and historical records of their knowledge of the most important fact in history, as well as the unequaled and divine message that we have in Christ. Luke definitely states that many "eyewitnesses" had committed to writing certain facts and teachings pertaining to Christ, and that he himself, after careful research, was writing to confirm the certainty of such vital truths (Luke 1:1–3). It is likely that some of these records to which Luke refers were made before the Savior was crucified. Some, no doubt, were brief accounts, possibly letters to relatives or friends, of particular events, such as a miracle or description of the reaction of friends or foes to what Jesus had said or done.

59

Such eyewitness accounts Luke and the other Gospel writers had access to, to a certain extent at least, when they gave the world these tremendously treasured writings. Of course, they also knew and interviewed many people who had seen and heard Christ.

The first of the Pauline epistles, many believe, is Galatians, written around A.D. 48, before the Jerusalem conference recorded in Acts 15. If the conference had preceded the writing of it, the apostle Paul would surely have made mention of its conclusions, for doing so would have been a clinching argument against Gentile believers' having to submit to circumcision.

Recent Confirmatory Evidence From the Papyri

It is rather ironic that the earliest New Testament fragment discovered among the papyri affirms the existence of the last and latest Gospel. This fragment, found in Egypt, consists of John 18:31–33,37,38, and was published by C. H. Roberst in 1935 *(An Unpublished Fragment of the Fourth Gospel).* It is a copy made close to A.D. 100, possibly from the manuscript that John himself had written. It furnishes unassailable and reliable proof of the dependability and preservation of the Gospel of John as we have it in Greek today; for the text of the fragment agrees word for word with the Nestle Greek New Testament text, which is in popular use at present. Here we have proof positive that the autograph copies of the New Testament have not been miscopied and that their words have been transcribed accurately and preserved generation after generation.

Other extraordinary confirmatory evidence that the books of the New Testament were written in the first century and that they were treasured as precious and authoritative is the discovery of *Egerton Papyrus 2.* It was purchased from a dealer in 1934 in a collection of papyri and consists of four fragmentary pages of sayings of Christ. It is evidently part of an unknown gospel, paraphrasing ideas expressed in our four Gospels. This phenomenal discovery is explored in Bell and Skeat's *Fragments of an Unknown Gospel and Other Early Christian Papyri,* 1935. It paraphrases the thought of no less than twenty-one verses occurring in the four Gospels. Just when it was written is uncertain. Perhaps its greatest historical value lies in the fact that it furnishes new and convincing evidence that all the Gospels were written before A.D. 100 and that the fourth Gospel could have been written by the apostle John.

The oldest manuscript we have of the Gospel of John, except the fragmentary parts just mentioned, is the *Bodmer Papyrus II,* dated around A.D. 200. It was found in Egypt in 1955 and contains the first fourteen chapters of the fourth Gospel, plus several fragments of other chapters in it. It is valuable and noteworthy as our oldest witness (by about 150 years) for clearing up difficult readings in two verses, concerning which there has been considerable uncertainty. In John 7:8, we read, "I go *not yet* up to the feast," instead of "I go *not* up to the feast." The manuscripts are almost equally divided on these readings, so much so that the Nestle Greek text in one edition has one and then in another the other reading. Now the scales are tipped decisively in favor of the words *not yet.* In John 7:52, *Bodmer Papyrus II* has inserted the Greek article before the word *prophet:* "See that *the* (not *a*) prophet does not rise out of Galilee." None of our translations inserts the article *the* here. However, the context definitely implies that the Messiah was being discussed. Other prophets had come from Galilee.

A flood of light has come upon the text of the New Testament through comparative study of thousands of ancient manuscripts, as well as from the papyri. The *Beatty Papyri* of the third century, which contain large sections of the New Testament, have proved very helpful. The science of textual criticism reveals that the copying of manuscripts has been so accurate that there is uncertainty about only one-thousandth part of the New Testament, and that no teaching of it now stands in jeopardy.

Before the end of the first century, every book of the New Testament was written and highly treasured, but these books had not yet been assembled in one volume. As churches learned that another church or churches had copies of a book that they did not have, they arranged to acquire a copy for themselves. Thus,

61

gradually all the New Testament books were assembled. This process was almost complete by the end of the second century.

From the ascension of Christ onward, the teachings and authority of Jesus had full recognition in all the churches. The chief work of the apostles and the other preachers was to so proclaim Christ and His teachings that their hearers would accept Him as Savior and Lord. His life and teaching illuminated, fulfilled, and outranked much of the Old Testament.

In worship services, parts of both the Old and New Testaments were customarily read. Both before and after the death of the apostles, their writings were highly treasured. Their oral and written testimony was regarded as the best and final authority as to what Christ had said and done. After their death, their writings more than ever were considered indispensable, as well as trustworthy and authoritative in all the churches.

As early as A.D. 95, Clement of Rome quoted freely from Matthew, Luke, Hebrews, Romans, Corinthians, and so forth, in his long letter to the Christians in Corinth. *The Epistles of Ignatius* (A.D. 115) have scores of quotations from the Gospels and the Pauline epistles (Eph. 5; Rom. 6,7). *The Epistle of Polycarp* to the Philippians (A.D. 120) makes extensive use of verses in Philippians and also cites nine of the other Pauline epistles, as well as ten of the other New Testament books. Not only have these and other contemporary writers quoted New Testament books as authoritative and inspired, but they have also given evidence that their whole philosophy of life was governed by the truths set forth in the New Testament (cf. *The Didache,* about A.D. 120; *The Shepherd of Hermas,* A.D. 130; *The Epistle of Barnabas,* A.D. 130). To the authors of such writings, the teachings of Christ and the apostles were authoritative and absolutely dependable in all matters of faith and Christian conduct. In *The Epistle of Barnabas,* we first find the phrase "it is written," referring to a New Testament book (IV. 14).

By A.D. 170, most, if not all, of the books of the New Testament were very likely being read on a par with Old Testament books. Their inherent quality of inspiration and authority, originated and motivated as they were by the Holy Spirit, led to their acceptance and acknowledgment. However, in some churches, a few "apocryphal" books, written in the second century, were also read at times. Certain heresies, such as Gnosticism, challenged the authority of the New Testament message and questioned the authenticity of some New Testament books. Such disagreement and conflicting views motivated Christian leaders to come to an understanding as to what books were to be regarded as most worthy and useful in the preservation and proclamation of Christianity. In *The Muratorian Fragment,* dated in the late second century, all the New Testament books are listed except 3 John, James, Hebrews, 1 and 2 Peter. Complete unanimity, evidently, had not yet been attained in the matter of the New Testament Canon.

In the fourth century, a few general epistles, especially 2 Peter, were still questioned by some, as well as the book of Revelation. In one of his pastoral letters, Athanasius (A.D. 296–373) included all twenty-seven books we now recognize. He wrote: "These are the wells of salvation so that he who thirsts may be satisfied with the sayings in these. Let no one add to these. Let nothing be taken away." In the Council of Carthage in 397, well attended by delegates from many churches, this declaration was made: "Aside from the canonical Scriptures, nothing is to be read in church under the name of divine Scriptures." The twenty-seven books in our New Testament were acknowledged as the only ones qualified to belong to the New Testament Canon.

Back of the choices made as to what books should receive this high recognition is this noteworthy fact: Whenever it was certain that an apostle had written a book, that book was deemed indispensable and was considered worthy to be a part of the Canon. The apostles had firsthand knowledge of what they wrote; they had had personal contact with Jesus of Nazareth. The next most authoritative writers would naturally be men who knew the apostles well and had often heard them give their testimonies. They were in an ideal and unique historical relationship to give reliable information as to the message and the interpretations given by the apostles.

Chapter 11

Baptism in the Dead Sea Manual of Discipline

Scholars are just beginning to explore the significant values of the Dead Sea Scrolls. Those found in the cave in Palestine northwest of the Dead Sea in 1947 were not translated into English and were not available until recently. Only a few months ago, the announcement was made of another discovery of scrolls, seventy in number, and several are fragmentary copies of Old Testament books, whereas in the 1947 discovery, only one Old Testament book was found, a copy of Isaiah. The prevailing opinion is that all these scrolls were stored away in caves in the first century B.C., but no one knows when the scrolls were copied from Old Testament books. For that reason, they are of tremendous value as witnesses of a text prevalent over 2,000 years ago.

In both discoveries, most of the manuscripts found were not extant in our generation and so are totally different and new to us; and they are sectarian in nature, writings apparently for the Essenes or "Sons of the New Covenant." Among them are the *Habakkuk Commentary,* the *Lamech Apocalypse,* the *Thanksgiving Psalms, The War of the Sons of Light with the Sons of Darkness,* and *The Sectarian Manual of Discipline,* which is abbreviated DSD. These throw considerable light on the Jewish customs and history of the period and also furnish a parallel for several statements in the New Testament. However, in this article, we are

64

focusing our attention exclusively on what is said about baptism in the DSD and its relation to similar references in the New Testament.

The Essenes, or "New Covenanters," did not participate in the rituals and ceremonies performed in Jerusalem. External rites were considered by them to be without value in spiritual development. Philo said that they served God "not by sacrificing animals but by seeking to order their thoughts in accord with holiness" (Quod omn. prob. lib., 575). Josephus (*Wars* II.8) stated that they subjected themselves to a more severe discipline than did either the Sadducees or the Pharisees and that they exceeded all others in virtue. Or, in other words, their emphasis was on real spiritual progress, on genuine righteousness, growth of the inner life, and was nonceremonial and nonsacramental. Josephus (*Wars* II.8.7) has also stated that would-be Essenes were carefully observed and kept on probation one year to ascertain the genuineness of their repentance and their progress in doing God's will before they were "made partakers of the waters of purification," which we believe meant baptism.

The DSD has specified many characteristics of holy living requisite for all who sought membership with the Essenes. They had to pledge themselves to be willing to repent from all sin and "to keep from all evil, to practice truth, justice and right . . . and not to take a single step outside the works of God." They were also required to make an open confession to this effect before the members of the organization.

> All those who enter into the rule of the community shall pass into the covenant in the presence of God (pledging) to act according to all that He has commanded them and not to depart far from Him through terror however great . . . though they be tempted by the whole empire of the Devil himself . . . Let him enter into the Covenant of God in the presence of all those who have bound themselves to it . . . with all his heart and with all his soul.

Whether this public confession of faith and loyalty was at

the beginning or end of the year of probation and whether it was followed by baptism, or the rite of bodily purification, we are not informed. But our surmise is that it was at the end of the year of probation. The first confession of intent may have been made before a small number of the community.

At any rate, the DSD does state that only the Spirit of God could cleanse one's soul and that "perverse men who walk in the way of wickedness . . . are not reckoned in His covenant" and that "they may not enter into water to touch the purity of holy men, for they will not be cleansed unless they have turned from their wickedness." The DSD goes on further to state that "He cannot purify himself by atonement, nor cleanse himself with water for impurity, nor sanctify himself with seas or rivers, nor cleanse himself with any water for washing." (Brownlee, *The Dead Sea Manual of Discipline,* iii, 4–5; v,13). Or, in other words, one's soul was supposed to have been cleansed by God before his body was cleansed by baptism. Thus, baptism was not considered a sacrament, but rather a symbol of a previous soul commitment to God, who alone could grant forgiveness of sins.

In the New Testament, we find a kindred emphasis upon the necessity of genuine repentance from sins, and upon having the fountains of one's heart and motives pure and noble. We have numerous statements that external religious rites are without value as a substitute for inward cleansing and righteousness. The Pharisees are condemned in scorching sentences for their dependence upon external rites and practices, as well as for their lack of inward righteousness.

The Gospels of Mark (1:4–8), Matt. (3:1–12), and Luke (3:1–20) depict John the Baptist giving specific details as to what he demanded of his hearers before baptism was administered. When the masses, or people as a whole, asked him, "What shall we do?" he said, "He who has two suits of underwear let him share with the one not having any; and the one who has food let him do likewise." When the tax collectors, who worked for the Roman government, came for baptism and asked, "Teacher what should we do?" he replied, "Stop collecting any more than is prescribed for you." Evidently officials, even in those times, had the notorious reputation of overtaxing people. When soldiers asked "What ought we to do?" he responded, "Never extort money from anyone, never make a false accusation, and always be satisfied with your wages." So drastic and severe was John in denouncing sin that he even dared to say, "You spawn of vipers, who warned you to flee from the coming wrath? Produce fruit that is evidence of repentance and don't begin to say We have Abraham as our father; for I say to you that God is able to raise up children for Abraham from these stones."

Carl Kraeling, who was president of the American Schools of Oriental Research and also director of the Oriental Institute of the University of Chicago, in his recent book entitled *John the Baptist,* has expressed some pertinent and significant ideas, as to the character and function of John's baptism. It is his belief that it was immersion in water. "Immersion being the most radical form of ablutionary procedure, the chances are that such a new rite created in this setting would involve a full bath and thus be the type of baptism John chose." (p. 113). He further affirms that Judaism never produced a rite that was efficacious of and by itself, hence a sacrament, and that it is doubtful whether John would have departed from the Jewish point of view in this particular. Baptism, in his estimation, was an act of self-humiliation before God, a voluntary expression of true repentance that resulted in divine forgiveness. If John's baptism then was an act expressive of genuine repentance, "it could mediate forgiveness without conferring it. It could mediate forgiveness without being a sacrament" (p. 121). Thus, baptism was the seal and sign of real repentance and of self-surrender to God.

If Dr. Kraeling has rightly interpreted the significance of baptism, we need then in Matt. 3:11 to accept such translations of John's statement as are found in Cooke's revision of Weymouth, or those occurring in Goodspeed's and Williams's translations, which in substance translate it "I indeed baptize you in water as an expression of repentance." They imply, by their translations, that the Greek preposition *eis,* which precedes *metanoian,* or repentance here, is causal in effect. A series of four articles in the quarterly, the *Journal of Biblical Literature,* during

1951 and 1952, deal with this question pro and con (Mantey versus Marcus).

Also, confirmatory of Dr. Kraeling's viewpoint is the expression "baptism of repentance," which occurs four times in the New Testament (Mark 1:4; Luke 3:3; Acts 13:24 and 19:4). Greek grammarians interpret the genitive construction here as being descriptive. Consequently, the full force of the expression signifies a baptism symbolic or expressive of repentance. Or, in other words, Christian baptism originally and in apostolic days was always to be preceded by thoroughgoing repentance. Prof. F. F. Bruce of England, in *Acts of the Apostles (1951),* says, "Baptism as an outward sign of repentance and remission of sins was no new thing in Judaism, and the command would occasion no undue surprise . . . Baptism was the outward and visible sign of inward and spiritual cleansing" (pp.97, 403).

Josephus, a first-century Jewish historian, in *Antiq.,* XVIII.5.2, has stated very clearly that John did require repentance before baptism, and also that baptism was not administered "in order to put away sins," but that it was "for the purification of the body, assuming that the soul was thoroughly purified beforehand." According to him, converts under the ministry of John the Baptist and neophyte Essenes were both carefully screened before being allowed to participate in the public rite of baptism or "purification of the body."

The publication of a translation of the *Manual of Discipline* occurred apparently after Dr. Kraeling had written his book. Otherwise, he could have quoted from it to substantiate his position. It apparently antedates both the New Testament and the writings of Josephus. It confirms Josephus' statement that each neophyte had to pledge himself to do God's full will and to demonstrate progress in doing so before participating in the public rite of bodily purification or baptism.

The Pharisaic emphasis on public and ceremonial rites was not shared by Christians of the first century, but it began to be accepted with reference to baptism in the second century when some leaders were declaring that it was necessary to salvation. In the light of the repeated and unified New Testament teachings on the necessity and importance of inward righteousness, is it not likely that the Essene rather than the Pharasaic emphasis is nearer to the spirit and practice of the early Christians? Baptism was, nevertheless, considered very important since Christ had commanded it and since it constituted the approved way of publicly confessing one's faith in and loyalty to Christ as well as being an initiatory rite to church membership (Acts 2:38).

Chapter 12

The Implication of the Greek Words for Baptism

Since the New Testament was first written in Greek and then translated into many languages from it, including the English, it is enlightening to ascertain what such words as *baptisma* (noun) and *baptizo* (verb) actually conveyed to the Greeks. Even today, in modern Greek, these words still are used as they were 2000 years ago and mean 'immersion,' and not pouring or sprinkling (cf. Sophocles,[1] *Modern Greek Dictionary*). No standard Greek dictionary has any statement to the contrary, and a dictionary is considered the final authority usually as to the meaning of a word.

A recent study has been completed by us of every occurrence of the words "baptize" and "baptism" in Greek in the extant works contemporary with the New Testament and in some works earlier and later, such as those written by Polybius, Strabo, Josephus, Philo, Plutarch, Epictetus, and Lucian. These studies reveal that these words were never used to imply pouring or sprinkling. Strabo, speaking of salty water, said, "for even those who cannot swim are not *immersed,* floating like pieces of wood"; "there is no need of being a swimmer, and he who enters in is not *immersed,* but is lifted out"; and in describing the rush of the Pyramus River in Asia Minor, he said, "the force of the water makes so much resistance, that it (an arrow) is hardly *immersed,* floating like wood''; and he tells of how Alexander's army "marched the whole day in water, *immersed* as far as up to the waist.''

Acts 22:16 needs to be translated "Arise, be baptised and have your sins washed away *by calling on his name.*'' The Greek participle for calling is passive and instrumental in usage here. Paul, for three days prior to his baptism, had been praying (Acts 9:11).

Note

1. For reference, see Greek dictionaries by Bauer, Cremer-Kogel, Kittel, Liddell, and Scott, Thayer, or Abbott Smith. In the scores of contexts in the New Testament and in other contemporary literature, we never found one instance where *baptize* was used in an iterative sense, in spite of Thayer's statement to that effect.

Chapter 13

Was Baptism Administered to Infants?

A careful reading of every passage in the New Testament on baptism will impress the intelligent reader with the fact that there are several differences between Holy Writ and current practices in many churches. Among the most striking divergences from this sacred authority is that of infant baptism.

Infant baptism has no authority for its existence, either in Scripture or in the practice of first-century Christianity. It is an inheritance that many Protestants have borrowed from the Roman Catholics. It seems to have grown out of the unscriptural teaching that baptism is necessary to salvation, a fallacy that began to develop gradually in the second century. Unfortunately, it contributes to filling churches with unregenerate members, many of whom have no interest in being Christians, do not attend church services or give of their means to support our Christian faith, and yet believe that their baptism guarantees them eternal life. In such circumstances, their baptism is a detriment and hindrance to the church and is a deceptive curse to themselves.

The first allusion in history to children (not babes) being baptized is found in Tertullian's treatise on baptism (chapter 18). This innovation apparently was just beginning to occur in a few churches at the beginning of the third century.

Therefore, according to the condition and disposition and age of each person, the delaying of baptism is more beneficial, especially in the case of little ones. . . . Let them come while they are growing up; let them come while they are learning, while they are being taught whither they are coming. Let them become Christians when they are able to know Christ. . . . Let them learn to desire salvation. . . . Such as understand the importance of baptism are more afraid of presumption than procrastination, and *faith alone secures salvation.*

From the above quotation, we learn (1) that Tertullian assumes that children up to the age of accountability were not considered sinners and, hence, without need of salvation; (2) that he favored deferring baptism for them until they were old enough to be taught the salient facts pertaining to Christ, and (3) that children should not be baptized until they of their own accord decided to become Christians—"let them learn to desire salvation."

Of course, since the prevalent form of baptism was immersion, children, regardless of how young, if and when they were baptized, were immersed. That is the only form of baptism ever practised by the Greek Orthodox Catholic Church as far back as their origin, and that goes back as far as the Roman Catholic Church. Immersion of infants, as well as of adults, is the practice of the Greek Orthodox Catholics. Knowing Greek, they have not been misled by faulty or ambiguous translations of *baptizo,* as most of Christendom has been. However, while we commend them for preserving the apostolic mode of baptism, we deplore the fact that they have departed from the apostolic practice of baptizing only believers.

The First Occurrence of Infant Baptism

The first unquestioned historical statement advocating the practice of infant baptism is found in Cyprian's *Letters* (lxvi) *to Fidus*. In answer to Fidus's question as to what age children may be baptized, Cyprian replied, after he had counseled with other pastors in Africa (c. A.D. 257), that "Infants are equal to men: but if you refuse to baptize them you destroy this equality, and are partial." He gave no quotation from the New Testament to support his recommendation for inaugurating this radical departure from the apostolic practice. Apparently, this decision on the part of those African Christian leaders in and around Carthage was opposed by Christians elsewhere for a long period of time, for they did not advocate it. Not until the fifth century do we have evidence of the practice elsewhere.

Augustine, also of North Africa (born A.D. 373), whose mother Monica refused to have him baptized until he became of age and would decide for himself to accept and follow Christ, became an ardent advocate of infant baptism and had considerable to do with Catholics everywhere accepting it as a church custom. However, the contemporary Donatists strenuously opposed its acceptance.

A fact often overlooked in discussing the origin of infant baptism is that the word infant (*infantulus* in Latin) was used also to denote a minor, or one who had not attained to a legal age. Robert Robinson in his *History of Baptism* (1790) has given convincing proof of this: "Now there are four unquestionable evidences that the words infant, child, and all other synonyms. . . .are used indiscriminately for minors. These evidences are manuscripts, books, inscriptions and laws" (page 140). He has cited several instances from inscriptions, wills, and other sources dated from about A. D. 500 to 1000 as positive proof. Here is a sample: "I, Adalb, the infant son of Waltper, being sick and in danger of death. . . .offer to God and to the Church of blessed St. Martin my house, etc. . . . Witness my hand, Adalb, who ordered this deed to be made."

Mr. Robinson stated that the ordinary infant baptism of Italy in the Middle Ages was the baptism of minors, who were taught before they were baptized and were supposed to be capable of choosing a religion (p. 141).

Current Opinion on Infant Baptism

A survey of the European writings on baptism during 1903–1928 reveals almost universal agreement that infant baptism did not develop until after the apostolic period, and that no scholar defended it as a New Testament rite. There is also agreement among these writers that baptism originally was for believers only. The one notable exception was Gustav Aulen, who ventured the guess that infant baptism existed in the primitive church. On the other hand, only Johannes Warns advocated the discontinuance of infant baptism.

However, beginning with 1928, claims were made by Joachim Jeremias, Abrecht Oepke, and others that infant baptism may have had its origin in the baptism of Jewish proselytes and was taken over by Christians from that source. However, confirmation for this assertion is lacking. R. Reitzenstein in his *Die Vorgeschichte der Christlichen Taufe,* 1929, pp. 188–389, has demonstrated the groundlessness of the claims that infants were baptized in primitive Christianity. So also has Hans Windisch, who argued that the apostles taught that (1) conversion preceded baptism; (2) that infants were innocent and therefore baptism would be of no value for them; (3) that baptism demands conscious conversion of sinful men and that it was preceded by instruction. He concluded that infant baptism could not have come into vogue before the last of the second century, if by then, and that it constituted defection from apostolic Christianity.

Arguments Pro and Con on Infant Baptism

Pedobaptists claim that the fact that the New Testament mentions the baptism of households implies that infants must have been included. But a careful reading of the context in every case gives no evidence that babies were baptized. The account of the baptism of Cornelius and his household (Acts 10:44–48) expressly states that only those were baptized who had received the Holy Spirit, having heard the Word preached by Peter. Those baptized also were heard "speaking in tongues and extolling God."

Chapter 14

Playing on Stringed Instruments

Since a few denominations refrain from instrumental music in their church programs of worship, on the grounds of their belief that the NT has nothing in its favoring instrumental music, we shall cite every reference in *koine* Greek writings, which we know of where *psallo,* meaning to *play on a stringed instrument,* is found. Some admit that it meant this prior to NT times, but claim that it lost that meaning and means only *to sing* in the NT.

Liddell, Scott and Jones in their Greek lexicon, which is the highest authority for non-biblical Greek, define the verb, "to pull and let go again with the fingers, usually to play a stringed instrument with the fingers, instead of with the plectrum"; and the noun *psalmos,* "the sound of the cithara, harp etc. . . later, a song sung to a stringed instrument, a psalm, LXX and N.T." The Abbott-Smith *Manual Greek Lexicon of the NT* defines the verb, "to play a stringed instrument with fingers . . . later, to sing to a harp, sing psalms (LXX)": and the noun, "a striking of musical strings . . . a sacred song sung to musical accompaniment, a psalm (LXX)."

Both the verb and noun occur frequently in the LXX and in accordance with the above definitions. For examples, we quote six verbal uses: Ps. 33:3, "Sing unto Him a new song, *play* well *upon* a *stringed instrument* with shouting." In 1 Sam. 16:16–18,23 "seek out a man to *play on a harp* . . . that he shall *play the harp* with his hand . . . a man that can *play the harp* well . . . is cunning in *playing the harp* . . . David took a harp *(kinuron)* and *played on it* with his hand *(epsallen en cheiri autou)."* Note the instrument is named, and it is stated that he played on it with his hand, not his mouth, i.e., he was not singing.

Since some are skeptical about this verb meaning to play on an instrument in NT times, we herewith cite several examples. But first we give a few instances of *psaltes,* a *harp* or *lyre player,* to help complete the picture on this subject: Strabo, *Geo.* 14.2.19 and 14.2.26, "the *harp player* . . . having many *harp players"*; Plutarch, *Morals* IV 334.1.C, "Philip once argued with a certain *psalten, harp player,* about the construction of his instrument." Note the harp players had musical instruments, as this last reference proves.

Both of the preceding authors quoted were of the first century; Strabo was born 63 B.C. and so antedates the NT, but he was at his height as a writer at the beginning of the first century A.D.; and Plutarch was born around A.D. 50 and was at his best in writing at about A.D. 100. We next quote from Philo, born 20 B.C. and a voluminous, first-century, religious writer: *Dreams* 1.7, "Furthermore heaven, the archetype musical instrument *(organon)* seems to be perfectly arranged for nothing else except that hymns, being   sung to the honor of the Father of all, may be *played on an instrument* musically *(adomenoi humnoi mousikos episallontai)."* Here it is stated that hymns are being sung with musical accompaniment. There is a separate word for hymn, another for singing *(adomenoi),* and a third for playing an instrument.

In returning to Plutarch again, we find these quotation: XI, *Aratus* 6.4, "talking with the women that were accustomed to *playing on the harp* and flute at banquets"; *Pericles* 1.5, "ashamed to *play an instrument?* It is enough surely if a king has leisure to hear others *play an instrument." Morals* III. 173.C, "but *to play the lyre* and the flute (psallein kai aulein)"; *Crassus* 32.5, "trailing off in the rear of the line into dances, cymbals, *harp-playing (psalmous)* and nocturnal revels with women."

Note that the noun is used here and that dancing, cymbal-sounding, and women are associated with playing the harp (or psalming). It certainly does not imply an atmosphere favorable for psalm-singing.

But Josephus, another first-century A.D. writer, gives us even more convincing evidence as to *psallo: Antiq.* Bk.VI.9.3, "a man who could play the harp . . . became divinely inspired at the *playing of the harp.*" In Bk.IX.13.3, "sang hymns to God and *played* their *harps*"; Bk.XII.323, "honoring God with songs of praise and the *playing of harps.*" (See also in the same book section 349 for the use of the noun.) In Bk.IX.13.2, "The Levites standing in a circle with their musical instruments *(mousikon organon)* sang hymns *(heydon humnous)* to God and *played on harps* (epsallon) as they had been taught by David." Such commands are common in the Psalms, e.g., 147:6, "Sing unto the Lord with thanksgiving, sing praise *upon the harp* unto our God." In 149:3, "sing praises unto him with the timbrel and *harp.*"

As conclusive proof that *psallo* still meant to play upon an instrument as late as the second century A.D., we quote from Lucian: *The Parasite.* 17, "And the other arts, moreover, cannot be of use to their possessor without instruments, for it is impossible to flute without flutes or to *play a lyre* without a lyre, *sallein aneu, luras,* or to ride a horse on horseback without a horse." Lucian states that it is not possible to *psallo* without a stringed instrument. Since one can sing without any kind of musical accompaniment, we are face to face with the fact that the word did not mean to sing here, but rather to *play on a lyre.*

With the foregoing as lexical historical background, let us translate the word in the NT in accordance with our findings. In Rom. 15:9, "I will *play on a stringed instrument* to thy name"; in 1 Cor. 14:15, "I will *play on a harp* with the spirit and with the mind"; in Eph. 5:19, "singing and *playing on instruments* with your hearts to the Lord"; in James 5:13, "Is anybody cheerful? Let him *play on a harp.*"

So we conclude that to *psallo* meant to play on a stringed instrument, usually on a harp or lyre. Since the NT commands us to do so, all the benefit of the doubt is in favor of those

79

worshipers who have musical instruments in their services. Since no evidence is available outside the NT that even remotely implies that *psalloing* might mean singing, we seem to have only positive, unimpeachable, and uncontradictable evidence to prove that to *psallo* meant to play on an instrument.

Paul commanded (Eph. 5:19) that we use spiritual songs (addressed to men), hymns (addressed to God), and that we sing these with musical accompaniment *(psallontes),* and with our hearts to God and that we be thankful. Church music then is to be sacred and soulful, not just for art's sake, but it is to be rendered with emotion to God in genuine worship. It is not for the glory of the musicians, but for the glory of God.

Chapter 15

Filled With the Spirit

The most magnificent event after Christ's ascension was the coming at Pentecost of the Holy Spirit into the lives of the disciples. Prophets had foreseen and declared it, and had themselves experienced it to a certain extent. For only a few people in any generation under the old dispensation had come under the mighty sway of God's Spirit. However, in the new dispensation, every true worshiper was to be so honored. As Joel and others had predicted, God would pour out his Spirit upon all flesh (Joel 2:28–32), and would write his law upon people's hearts and minds, so much so that none would need to say to another "know the Lord" (Heb. 8:10–11).

At that point in the history of the world, God on a grand scale began indwelling every true believer, and in doing so, he began making himself available and near to every responsive individual. This was an unprecedented and an unparalleled revolutionary change. Beginning here, the resources of heaven are put at the disposal of all disciples. The divine at last is put within reach of the human. The authority and power of heaven that Jesus said was his is freely distributed to humble, insignificant, and even uneducated followers. Even poverty-stricken people with no social standing whatever, such as slaves, began being filled with the Spirit and became, as a consequence, zealous, powerful, and persuasive witnesses for Christ. God took the people at the bottom of the social ladder and raised them to an equal status with those at the top of ladder, in respect to this privilege. Since about 50 percent of the people in the Roman empire were slaves and had very few rights, this offer from God to elevate them to equality with others by making them his children, upon their acceptance of Christ as Savior, was news of tremendous significance.

What did it mean for the disciples? First of all, it meant assurance of salvation. "The Spirit bears witness with our spirit that we are children of God" (Rom. 8:16). Second, it meant divine power to help overcome trials and temptations. "God is faithful who will not permit you to be tempted beyond what you are able but with the temptation will also make the way of escape that you may be able to endure it" (1 Cor. 10:13). Third, it meant guidance from God in making the best possible decisions. Philip was led to a highway to meet and introduce to Christ the distinguished treasurer of the faraway Ethiopian government. Ananias, under God's direction, had the rare privilege of instructing and baptizing Saul, who became the most successful exponent of Christianity of that generation, if not of all generations. The same Spirit is waiting to guide people today as to vocations, marriage, business ventures, and a thousand and one other decisions, major or minor, that must be made. Fourth, receiving the Spirit meant effectiveness as to service. Examples in the New Testament of such help are numerous.

The 120 disciples at Pentecost were used of God, in spite of Jerusalem being the chief center of opposition against Christianity, so much so that its leaders had had Jesus crucified, so that they became such bold and eloquent witnesses that 3000 people pledged allegiance that day to accept and follow Christ. Peter and John, a few days later on, defied the Sanhedrin, when instructed to keep silent about Jesus' resurrection from the dead, by saying, "We must obey God rather than men." Paul, after years of experience in enjoying the benefits of the Spirit's presence and power in his life, said "I can do all things through Christ who strengthens me," and "My God will supply every need of yours according to his riches in glory in Christ Jesus'' (Phil. 4:13, 19).

In fact, the resources of heaven were so near and so real and so powerful that no barrier or obstacle could cope with them. Sickness and deformities were cured when people prayed, demons were cast out, prison doors were opened, and even the dead were brought back to life (Acts 5:12–20; 9:40).

The expression 'baptized by the Spirit' seems to have meant the same as receiving the Spirit or as being filled with the Spirit. These terms simply signify the fact that people turned their lives over to God to live and serve as he desired and directed, and as a consequence received guidance, courage, power, etc., from God. We are informed in Acts 5:32 how we may become filled with the Spirit, ''the Holy Spirit whom God has given to those that obey him.'' Notice the sole condition mentioned is obedience. The Greek tense conveys the idea of continuance in obedience, i.e., as long as we are fully yielded to God and busy for him, so long does he continue filling us with his Spirit. In fact, we are commanded (Eph. 5:18) ''to continue being filled with the Holy Spirit.'' To realize this marvelous and heavenly privilege, we place ourselves at God's disposal as willing servants seeking to further his will and, in doing so, to help enrich the lives of those whose lives we touch. Some disciples were filled again and again for specific tasks or difficulties. So real was this experience of divine fellowship and power that, in Acts alone, the Holy Spirit is mentioned sixty-three times. A few references to how the Spirit helped people are: Acts 1:8; 2:4; 4:8,31; 6:3,5; 9:17; 13:9, 52; 18:25. Peter and Paul, especially, are mentioned as having been filled with the Spirit on more than one occasion, and each time the result was effectiveness in witnessing for Christ.

However, not only is obedience specified as a prerequisite to having the Spirit's presence and power, but also prayer. Pentecost did not come, with its pouring out of the Spirit on the disciples, until after ten days of earnest and sincere soul-searching prayers (Acts 1:14). The next reception of the Spirit by the church also came after a season of prayer (4:31). The Samaritan Christians did not receive the Spirit until after prayer for them and by them (8:15–17). That condition must be met by us if we desire similar results. Jesus said God stands ready to give his Spirit to those that ask for him, just as parents stand ready to give good gifts to their children. When we have his guidance, comfort, and assurance. In other words, heaven's doors are opened to us, and its blessings and resources become available to us to the extent that we claim them and need them.

However, the one prime purpose mentioned in connection with giving his Spirit to us is to enable and equip us to become adequate and persuasive witnesses for him, that we may become the channels of his matchless grace in persuading others to join us in worshiping and serving him. "But you shall receive power when the Holy Spirit has come upon you; and you shall be my witnesses in Jerusalem . . . and to the end of the earth" (Acts 1:8). Can anything be more satisfying and worthwhile than winning a person to Christ? If so, I have never found it. I'd rather have such a record to my credit than anything else. Wouldn't you?

Chapter 16

The Divine Election

The Biblical teachings on election are so intricately interwoven into the whole fabric of the Bible that they are inseparable from it and very much a distinct and vital part of it. According to Emil Brunner,[1] election constitutes the center and core of the teachings of the Old and the New Testaments.

The Apostle Paul implies that the doctrine was so important that God had it in mind before He created the universe. "He chose us in him before the foundation of the world, that we should be holy and without blemish before him in love . . . for we are his workmanship, created in Christ Jesus for good works."[2] Or, in other words, God through Christ, even before man was created, had a redemptive program for man, which anticipated a favorable response from man, expressed by blameless character and loving service.

Calvin's over-emphasis on the negative aspect of predestination (although it is not synonymous with election) contributed toward bringing the whole doctrine of election more or less into disrepute. The gist of his viewpoint is summarized in this quotation from his *Institutes:* "By an eternal and immutable counsel God has once for all determined, both whom he would admit to salvation and whom He would condemn to destruction . . . God

85

favors His elect because He will and has mercy because He will.''[3]

While the apostle Paul did say, ''He hath mercy on whom he will, and whom he will he hardeneth,''[4] he nevertheless did not apparently, have in mind, according to the context, God's dealings with men as a whole, but rather chiefly with Pharaoh, whom God used to make the lot of the Israelities so unbearable in Egypt that they would gladly follow Moses' leadership and seek to escape from their unendurable bondage. When Paul speaks of ''vessels of wrath,'' he seems to be referring to various nations that God used at different times to discipline Israel, the ''vessel of mercy.''[5] He was not discussing unredeemed individuals, apparently. The basic thought, emphasized by Paul, was that God's decisions and choices should never be questioned, since His character and love would always impel Him to do right. His sovereignty, therefore, should never be impugned.

The New Testament certainly has many statements that teach that God was not predestinating anyone to destruction, but rather that He was always motivated by infinite love, and was seeking to redeem man and to elevate him to fellowship with Himself. The apostle John says: ''God sent not the Son into the world to judge the world; but that the world should be saved through him.''[6] And in speaking of the efficacy of Christ's death, he affirms that ''He was the propitiation not for our sins only but also for the whole world.''[7] Or in other words, God's grace has made redemption possible for every man. But since God has created man free, God cannot coerce man to serve Him, even by His infinite love, without infringing upon man's freedom. Christ stands at the crossroads of life. Choosing Him brings God's favor forever; rejecting Him brings God's disfavor forever! J.K.S. Reid says God's gracious offer of mercy is so generous that ''All are predetermined to election.''[8] ''God was in Christ reconciling the world unto Himself.''[9] But man must cast for himself the vote that decides the election. There is some merit in a Negro minister's explanation of the doctrine: ''God votes for you. The Devil votes against you. Then you vote, and you decide the election.'' God's readiness to forgive and redeem can be thwarted by man's recalcitrance and impenitence. Even divine love is expressed in vain when it does not enlist response and cooperation in man.

The Election of a Nation

According to the Genesis account, although God had chosen and signally blessed many individuals, from earliest antiquity and onwards, the most significant manifestation of an unbroken sequence of chosen men begins with Abraham, who is informed that he is to become the father of a multitude, the founder and forefather of a new type of nation. "All the nations of the earth shall be blessed in him."[10] His seed is to become as numerous as the sands of the sea and the stars of heaven. But these far-reaching and awe-inspiring promises were not made to Abraham unconditionally. "Walk before me and be thou perfect,"[11] the record reads. "And I will make my covenant between me and thee, and will multiply thee exceedingly."[12] Abraham was directed to command his children . . . "that they keep the way of Jehovah, to do righteousness and justice; to the end that Jehovah may bring upon Abraham that which he hath spoken of him."[13]

And God's declaration of readiness to bless Isaac begins with the condition that Isaac be submissive to God's will: "Go not down into Egypt. Dwell in the land which I shall tell thee of . . . and I will be with thee and bless thee . . . and I will establish the oath which I swore unto Abraham thy Father."[14] From these statements, we learn that the election is never merely automatic and unconditional. A covenant with God required renewal by each succeeding generation or it became invalid. However, the Old Testament writers never state nor imply that it was man's worth that elicited God's favor, but rather that it was God's gracious generosity that put the elect under constant obligation to serve God. This is recognized in Jacob's charge to his household when he said: "Let us arise, and go to Bethel; and I will make there an altar unto God, *who answered me in the day of my distress and was with me in the way which I went.*"[15]

In discussing God's choice of Jacob, H. H. Rowley has well

said: "Sometimes God chooses those who are not particularly choice. This is not the demonstration of His arbitrariness, but of His wisdom and His grace . . . For the character that he came to attain Abraham was chosen; Isaac and Jacob less for themselves than for those who should come after them.''[16]

And Israel as a nation was not chosen because she was better than other nations. "Rather it was the miracle of Divine grace that God chose her in her weakness and worthlessness and lavished His love upon her.''[17] "Jehovah thy God hath chosen thee to be a people for his own possession . . . Ye were the least of all people. It was because Jehovah loved you . . . that he redeemed you out of the house of bondage from the hand of Pharaoh, King of Egypt.''[18] Israel's greatness was due to God's goodness. But God not only chose Israel, but also claimed her for service. And the elect community realized that this claim was valid and concurred in it by ratifying the covenant at Mount Sinai, in which she agreed to obey and serve God wholeheartedly. Moses came and called for the elders of the people, and set before them all these words which Jehovah commanded him: and all the people answered together, and said, "All that Jehovah hath spoken we will do.''[19] Here because God has delivered Israel, she pledges herself to Him. Her election is seen to be, not something automatic that made her His people for all time by mere physical generation. But, on the contrary, we see that she entered into the covenant voluntarily, and each generation to become eligible for its benefits had to renew it by accepting for itself its obligations, which meant the doing of God's will, or it would place itself outside the covenant. It was man's response to divine grace, and only the heirs of response could be the heirs of the covenant.[20] Repudiation of the covenant by Israel released God from obligation to her. The promises that went with the election were binding on God only so long as, and while Israel obeyed God. But He, in spite of Israel's waywardness and stiff-neckedness, lavished His favor upon her, generation after generation. His love motivated Him to do far beyond what He had agreed to do. God's patience often postponed His punishments, which nevertheless came in the form of invasions, famines, diseases, and disasters of many kinds, and finally captivity.

Discipline for Disobedience

When the nation, groups in the nation, or individuals violated their covenant with God, they became liable to the extent of their sins. All that escaped from Egypt perished in the wilderness, except Caleb and Joshua. The rebellion of Korah resulted in immediate externation of Korah and his many followers.[21] Achan's theft resulted in speedy elimination of himself and his family. Thus, God sought to teach the divine community that His election of them would be favorable to them only to the extent that they kept faith with Him and serve Him constantly and consistently. Isaiah reminded them of this when he said: "Who gave Jacob for a spoil, and Israel to the robbers? Did not Jehovah, he against whom we have sinned?"[22] And he even predicted that the curse of God would be upon them and that God would switch His favor to non-Jews: "And ye shall leave your name for a curse unto my chosen; and the Lord Jehovah will slay thee; and he will call his servants by another name (Christian?): so that he who blesseth himself in the earth shall bless himself in the God of truth."[23]

So we see, all through the Old Testament, the recognition that Israel's election involved obligation for Israel, "and that the repudiation of those obligations was tantamount to the repudiation of the election."[24] The severe denunciation against the divine community by Amos and other prophets were due solely to Israel's violation of its covenant with God.

And Paul's statement in the New Testament in Romans 11:26, "all Israel shall be saved," needs to be interpreted in the light of Israel's historical background prior to Paul's day as well as in the light of all that Paul wrote with reference to Israel. Since the quotation is not preceded by an inferential conjunction, but rather by a correlative adverb of manner *(houtos),* and followed by a correlative adverb of comparison *(kathos),* it should not be translated, "So all Israel shall be saved," but rather, *"After this manner* will all Israel be saved," just as it is written, "There shall come out of Zion a Deliverer; He shall turn ungodliness away from Jacob." (Very likely Paul meant that Christ in His first coming was the Deliverer.) Or in other words, when Israel, or any Israelite turns away from ungodliness and instead turns his life and allegiance over to Christ, then those people will be saved, after the same manner as any other sinner can be saved. The New Testament does not appear to cherish the hope expressed by Jeremiah that Israelities from all nations would return to Palestine. It rather placed stress upon *what* we are before God rather than *where* we are or who our parents were. All boundaries of race and place as well as differences in color, were removed at the cross. Christians accepted as authoritative Jesus' pronouncement on this when He said, "Neither in this mountain, nor in Jerusalem, shall ye worship the Father . . . But the hour cometh, and now is, when the true worshippers shall worship the Father in spirit and truth: for such doth the Father seek to be his worshippers."[25]

Israel's Mission to the World

Although the Israelities were supposed to demonstrate righteous and exemplary character, and to enlist the Gentile nations about them in worshiping Jehovah, the Creator of the universe, they nevertheless seem to have failed almost utterly in the latter. Isaiah called their attention to this purpose of God for them: "I, Jehovah, have called thee in righteousness, and will hold thy hand, and will keep thee, and give thee for a covenant of the people, *for a light of the Gentiles . . . I will also give thee for a light to the Gentiles,* that thou mayest be my salvation unto the end of the earth."[26] The book of Jonah gives one conspicuous example of God's concern for the inhabitants of the Gentile city Nineveh. But the Jews apparently did not seriously accept the role for themselves of persuading the world to worship and serve Jehovah. However, involuntarily, through frequent dispersions and captivities, they did help considerably to prepare the way for the extension of Christianity.

An Elect Remnant

Although the prophets by the time Judah was taken into captivity (586 B.C.) had decided that Israel's election had ended in failure, they nevertheless still retained hopes that at least a remnant would remain in God's favor. They prophesied that those, and only those, that accepted the obligations of loyalty to God, were the true heirs of the election and that they alone would escape the severe chastisement of Jehovah. All through Israel's history, only a minority of the nation, with the possible exception of the early period of the wilderness wandering, kept its covenant with God. The majority regularly and repeatedly ignored or spurned Him. And so it has been with every nation and generation of people down to the present time. Man's perversity seems always to resist God's purpose and provision for man.

Isaiah frequently speaks of only·a remnant returning to Palestine. "A remnant shall return, the remnant of Jacob, unto the mighty God. For though thy people, Israel, be as the sand of the sea, only a remnant of them shall return."[27] And Isaiah narrows down this select group to only a part of one tribe by saying: "The remnant from the house of Judah that escapes shall again take root downwards and shall bear fruit upwards."[28] And Isaiah further states, "the remnant shall be very small and of no account."[29] Jeremiah, and several of the minor prophets agree with Isaiah that it will be a disciplined and a repentant remnant that will return to Jerusalem.[30] But Ezekiel conceives of a new, and a regenerate Israel: "I will give them another heart, and a new spirit will I put in their midst . . . that they may walk in my statutes and keep my commandments."[31] And he attributes the transformation in their character to the grace and mercy of God. This vision however, finds fulfillment only after the coming of Christ and in the reign of the Holy Spirit in men's lives.

Elect Individuals

God in Old Testament times selected a nation as the object of His favor and as a channel for His revelation. And after that nation spurned His reign over them, He chose that small group within the nation, the remnant, that was responsive to His leadership. But God also elected outstanding individuals, such as Abraham, Moses, Gideon, David, and the numerous prophets. These men and many others like them, received God's revelation, exemplified His character, sought to do His will and to serve the people of their generation. David expressed well what men of every generation need to feel and to express, when he prayed, "Create in me a clean heart, O God; and renew a right spirit within me."[32] Election to these stalwart leaders never meant arbitrary and blind favoritism. They knew and taught that they were obligated, because of God's grace and mercy, to reflect God's character within their own lives and to further God's will by service to others.[33] Apparently, they were very much aware that they would forfeit God's favor if they did not serve Him, for David prayed, "Cast me not away from thy presence; and take not thy Holy Spirit from me."[34]

But this emphasis upon individualism comes to full fruition only in the New Testament. The Christians alone are counted as the heirs of the election, and they are considered to be the true successors of Abraham. Abraham's physical descendants no longer had any monopoly on God's favor due to their nonconformity to His will. John the Baptist bluntly and courageously informed the Jews that being children of Abraham no longer had validity with God and that it did not guarantee God's pardon and peace; that God could even raise up children to Abraham from stones. They were sternly warned that unless they repented and showed fruits expressive of repentance, they would remain forever outside the pale of God's protection and pardon. But to those that came to John for baptism with humility and in the right spirit, he said: "I baptize you in water because of repentance but he that cometh after me is mightier than I . . . he will baptize you with the Holy Spirit and fire."[35] And Matthew quotes Jesus as saying, "The Kingdom of God shall be taken away from you and it shall be given to a nation that bringeth forth its fruit."[36] That statement fits in with what Jesus said when informed that His mother and brothers were outside the crowd seeking to talk with Him. He disclaimed the value of physical and family relationship by saying: "Behold, my mother and my brothers! For whosoever shall do the will of my Father who is in heaven, he is my brother, and sister, and mother."[37]

The Church, the Divine Community

Luke and Paul both quote Jesus as having said: "This cup is the new covenant in my blood."[38] The early church interpreted this statement as connected with and as a fulfillment of Jeremiah's prophecy of the new covenant: "I will write my law on their hearts" (31:33). These first-century Christians believed that Christ's Church superseded Israel and that the new covenant made invalid the old covenant.[39]

It seems beyond dispute that Paul thought of the Church as the true and only remnant of God. "They are not all Israel which are of Israel," he said. He contrasted the "Israel according to the flesh" with the "Israel of God," the Church of Christ.[40] In Romans, the idea is made more personal: "For he is not a Jew who is one outwardly, neither is that circumcision which is outward in the flesh; but he is a Jew who is one inwardly, and circumcision is that of the heart" (2:28f). To the Galatians, who were mostly Gentiles, Paul said: "Now we, brethren, are children of promise, as Israel was" (4:28f). But Paul develops the idea even further by teaching the Galatians: "If ye are Christ's then ye are the seed of Abraham, and heirs of the promises" (3:29). In Philippians 3:6, the Gentile Christians were informed: "For we are the true circumcision, who worship God in spirit, and who glory in Christ Jesus, and have no confidence in the flesh." And in writing to the Christians in Rome, Paul said: "We are the children of God; and if children, then, heirs, heirs of God, and fellow-heirs with Christ."[41]

In the first epistle of Peter, Christians, not Jews, were called "an elect race, a royal priesthood, a holy nation, a special people."[42] The promises to Israel as recorded in Exodus 19:5, are here claimed for the Church. Christians have inherited the peculiar relationship, privileges and benefits that were once the sole possession of the Israelites.

All through the New Testament the term "elect" means believers in Christ. They are spiritual Israel, the seed of Abraham, the true remnant, the heirs of God, Christ's brothers and sisters, "built upon the foundation of the apostles and prophets, Christ Jesus himself being the chief cornerstone."[43]

H. H. Rowley[44] points out that the Church not only claimed to be the heir of Israel's election but she also accepted the obligation of Israel's mission which was that she should, (1) share God's revelation with all humanity; (2) that she reflect the will and character of God in life; and (3) that, in a spirit of self-sacrificing love, she serve and help the needy wherever and whenever possible. "If He is the Servant . . . then also is the Church called to enter into the task of the Suffering Servant . . . The task of the Servant was to suffer. The Church is therefore called to enter the sufferings of the Cross in some measure, and to agaonize for the world's redemption . . . The Biblical doctrine of election is therefore penetrated through and through with warning. To be the elect of God is not to be His pampered favorite. It is to be challenged to a loyalty and a service, and a sacrifice that knows no limits."

Notes

1. *The Christian Doctrine of God*, 1950, p. 303.
2. Eph. 1:4; 2:10.
3. *Institutes* 3: 21-7; 3: 22-8.
4. Rom. 9:17-18.
5. Rom. 9:22-23.
6. John 3:17.

7. John 2:2.
8. *Scottish Journal of Theology*, Vol. I, No. 2.
9. 2 Cor. 2:19.
10. Gen. 18:18.
11. Gen. 22:17.
12. Gen. 17:1–2.
13. Gen. 18:19.
14. Gen. 26:2–3.
15. Gen. 35:3.
16. *The Biblical Doctrine of Election*, 1950, p. 35.
17. H. H. Rowley, p. 78.
18. Deut. 7:7–8.
19. Exod. 19:7–8.
20. H. H. Rowley, p. 48f.
21. Num. 16:20–35.
22. Isa. 42:24; 63:10.
23. Isa. 65:15–16.
24. H. H. Rowley, p. 69.
25. John 4:21–23.
26. Isa. 42:6; 49:6; 66:18–20.
27. Isa. 10:20–22.
28. Isa. 37:31.
29. Isa. 16:14b.
30. Jer. 23:3; Ezek. 14:22; Amos 5:15; Micah 5:3; Zeph 3:13.
31. Ezek. 11:19f; 14:22; 36:22–25.
32. Ps. 51:10.
33. As to the significance of faith, covenant, and confession for Christians cf. *The Review and Expositor*, Vol. XLVIII, April 1951, p. 169, "Inadequately Translated Words in the New Testament" by Mantey.
34. Ps. 51:11.
35. Matt. 3:11. On *eis = because of* here cf. "The Causal Use of EIS in the New Testament," in *Journal of Biblical Literature*, Vol. LXX, Part I, 1951.
36. Matt. 21:43. Cf. also Matt. 8:11.
37. Matt. 12:49.
38. Lk. 22:2; 1 Cor. 11:25.
39. Heb. 8:8–12; 2 Cor. 3:4–6; *diatheke* means agreement 31 times in the N. T. to only 2 meaning a will.
40. Rom. 9:6; 1 Cor. 10:18; Gal. 6:16.
41. Rom. 8:16–17.
42. 1 Pet. 2:9.
43. Eph. 2:20.
44. Rowley, pp. 161–168.

Chapter 17

Every Christian a Prophet

Most people seem to have the mistaken idea that the words 'prophet' and 'prophesy' meant primarily 'to foretell' in the Bible. However, Paul's usage of these words in 1 Cor., Chapter 14, does not fit into such a meaning. Verse 31 reads, "For you are all able to prophesy in order that all may learn and all be exhorted." Paul states the purpose of prophesying, namely, that people may learn and be comforted or exhorted. To foretell events accurately isn't a common experience, and even if it were, would it teach and edify people morally and spiritually, as Paul is writing about in the context? Would it convict and convert sinners as Paul visualized (v. 24)? Does it bring "edification, exhortation and consolation" (v. 3)? However, if we interpret these words in accordance with their prevalent usage in Greek literature, we become aware that Paul was here writing chiefly about witnessing for Christ and the proclamation of his Gospel, or forthtelling rather than foretelling.

L. S. and Jones have for the verb: "in the N. T., gift of expounding Scripture, or of speaking and preaching under the influence of the Holy Spirit" and for the noun: "one who speaks for a god and interprets his will to man." Such a definition accords with this example from Plutarch (*Lives* I (Loeb) p. 339): "the Pontifex Maximum had the duty of *expounding* the divine will, or rather of directing sacred rites.'' In agreement with such usage are most of the occurrences of the words meaning prophet or prophesy in both the OT and the NT, according to Paul Wells, who wrote a B.D. thesis on their biblical meanings. He found that the Hebrew words for prophecy mean foretelling only 64 times to 291 times meaning forthtelling.

However, in several passages, there is a combination of both ideas. As to the NT usage, he states: ''The noun prophecy is used 3 times in the N.T. and each time refers to forthtelling. The verb prophesy occurs 27 times, 5 times referring to foretelling and 22 times to forthtelling. The word prophet occurs 37 times meaning a foreteller and 107 times as a forthteller. We might define the prophet as God's spokesman or forthteller who delivers God's message.'' Paul declared that everyone of us can do this.

Chapter 18

Expectation or Glory

"All have sinned and fall short of the glory, *doxa*, of God." So read the R. and R.S. versions. There is no question but that *doxa* means glory most of the time in the NT, but it is just the reverse outside the NT. We found this ratio of usage: *Reputation,* 114 times; *opinion* or *expectation,* 68 times; *glory,* 58 times; *fame* 35 times. So it had other meanings by nearly four to one. In Plutarch, *Lives* III, F. *Maximus* 5.6, "frightened from one's course by the *opinions* of men"; ibid. *Nicias* 18.5, "for the *opinion* gained ground and strength"; ibid. VIII, *Cato the Younger* 69.2, "cast away these old *opinions* and arguments."

Thus, to fall short of God's glory means to fail to come up to God's *opinion, expectation,* or *standard of conduct* for us. He has a goal in mind, a blueprint for our lives, but all of us are guilty of having come short of that perfect pattern. However, our case is far from hopeless if we accept Christ who has made peace possible for us with God through his death.

Chapter 19

Ruler of Creation

In spite of the fact that nearly all NT translators translate *arche beginning* in Rev. 3:14, there is plenty of usage within and without the NT for translating the word *ruler* in this context, "These things says the Amen, the faithful one and true witness, the *ruler* or supervisor of the creation of God." This translation fits in with several NT statements: Rev. 1:5, "the firstborn of the dead, and the ruler *(archon)* of the kings of the earth." In Heb. 1:2, "through whom also he made the worlds *(aionas)* . . . upholding all things by the word of his power." In Col. 1:16,17, "for in him were all things created, in the heavens and upon the earth . . . and in him all things consist or hold together."

Arche is translated with the idea of *ruler* or person in authority in the following passages in the R. and the R.S. versions: Luke 12:11, "And when they bring you before synagogues and *rulers* and authorities"; Rom. 8:38, "nor angels, nor *principalities (archai)"*; Eph. 3:10, "to the intent that now unto the *principalities* and the powers in the heavenly places." In 6:12, "For our wrestling is not against the world rulers of this darkness"; in Tit. 3:1 "Remind them to be subject to *rulers,* to authorities, to be obedient." The same translation would also fit better in the context of Col. 1:18, "who is the *ruler,* the first born from the dead, that in all things he might have the preeminence." (So Bauer and Kittel)

Without question, other translations are more prevalent, properly, both in the NT and in other *koine* literature. Outside the NT, we found the following ideas expressed by the word: *Beginning* or *source,* eighty-seven times; *authority,* forty times; *office,* thirty-six times; *ruler* or *commander,* thirty-two times; *realm* or *dominion,* eighteen times. A few samplings of the usage as *ruler* are: Plutarch, *Morals* II.151.F, "he held the greatest and the most perfect position as a *ruler.*" In *Lives* VIII, *Sertorius* 10, "They were altogether lacking in a *commander* of great reputation." In *Morals* V.75.E, "For it is not fitting for the *Ruler* and Lord of all to listen to anyone." In *Diodorus Siculus* II Bk. 3.5.1, "him the multitudes take for their *king.*" In Philo, *Alleg.* III.58, "for the sake of being a *ruler* with governors"; 66, "Amalek, the *ruler* of the nations."

We have cited enough evidence to indicate the frequency of this type of translation in *koine* Greek and to point the way for its application in more NT passages. Abbott-Smith does not mention this meaning at all, but Liddell and Scott do. It is possible that *arche* means *the preeminent one* in John 8:25 instead of *at all,* which Abbott-Smith suggests.

Dr. Wikgren's suggestion that *arche* means *essentials* in Mark 1:1 finds partial support in Epict. 1:19.15, where the translator has rendered it *principle,* "the same principle will be for all." A similar usage occurs in Julian's *Orations* VII.225 D, "the *first principle* (i.e., *chief thing*) is to know thyself." In accord with these findings, Mark 1:1 can be translated, "the essentials (chief things) of the Gospel of Jesus Christ."

Chapter 20

Sodomy

The word *Malakos,* which literally means *soft* and is so translated
in Matt. 11:8; and Luke 7:25 is applied to clothes, implying
costly clothing, and is used similarly outside the NT. However,
it also has derogatory implications in non-NT sources and, when
applied to men, means *weak,* as in Plutarch, *Lives* III. 27.4,
"Artemon was very luxurious in his life as well as *weak* or
effeminate." But in 1 Cor. 6:9, the word is used in a metaphorical
sense, denoting sexual looseness of some kind.

Strange to say, we often hear people called soft who are
lacking in character. However, the fact that this word occurs in
this context between two others that mean sexual vice is strongly
suggestive that it also denotes a particular type of immorality:
"neither adulterers nor *sodomites* nor homosexuals" (the latter
word occurs in the R.S. version with the footnote, "Two Greek
words are rendered by this expression") shall inherit the kingdom
of God." The noun form, which in the NT, is used three times
meaning *weakness* or *disease,* Matt. 4:23; 9:35; and 10:1, has
the connotation also frequently of moral weakness and cowardice
outside the NT, is also used in Philo, *Abraham,* 26, to denote
some sort of sexual satisfaction of males with males: "And so,
by degrees the men became accustomed to be treated like women,
and in this way engendered among themselves the diseases of

females, an intolerable evil. For they not only feminized their bodies by means of *sodomy* and dissipation but they also made their souls ignoble, corrupting in this way the whole race of men.'' This reminds us of Paul's accusation of the men of the same generation, Rom. 1:27, ''likewise also the men, leaving the natural use of the woman, burned in their lust one toward another, men with men working unseemliness and receiving in themselves that recompense of their error which was due.''

Chapter 21

Age Connotations

In reading Philo's book, *Creation,* we were greatly delighted to discover a quotation from Hippocrates, the alleged founder of medical ethics, who lived c. 460 B.C. In this quotation, Hippocrates has given us the age connotations of seven Greek words, five of which occur in the New Testament. Although the New Testament writers did not always use these words in as technical and restricted sense as Hippocrates did, nevertheless, knowledge of his use of the terms throws light upon and adds color to several passages.

In man's nature there are seven hours (periods), which men call ages; little child, child, boy, and the rest. He is a *paidion* until he is seven, the time of shedding teeth. And he is a *pais* until puberty, until twice seven. And he is a *meirakion* until the growth of a beard, up to thrice seven. And he is a *neaniskos* up to the full development of all the body, until four times seven. And he is an *aner* up to fifty, lacking one, until seven times seven. And he is a *presbutes* up to fifty-six, until seven times eight. And after that he is a *geron.*

According to these age denotations, in the following passages, children from one to seven are mentioned: Matt. 11:16, children playing in the market; Matt. 18:2–5; Mark 9:36, 37; 10:13–15, children used to illustrate proper Christian attitudes; Mark 7:30, the daughter of the Syrophoenician woman; Mark 9:24, the demonized boy whom the disciples could not help; John 4:49, the nobleman's son whom Jesus healed.

Children from the age of seven to fourteen are referred to in the following passages: Matt. 8:6, the centurion's paralyzed boy; Luke 2:43, Jesus lost in Jerusalem; Luke 7:7, the centurion's sick servant; Luke 8:51, the daughter of Jairus; Acts 20:12, the boy who fell out of the window while Paul preached. But the word *pais* occasionally means only a descendant of, Matt. 2:16; 12:18; 17:18; and may frequently be translated as servant, Acts 3:13,26; 4:25,27,30. In these latter passages, it refers to adults.

Hippocrates' word for young men from twenty-one to twenty-eight is found in Matt. 19:20, 22, the rich young ruler; Luke 7:14, the son of the widow of Nain; Acts 23:18, Paul's nephew, who warned him of the plot against his life.

Chapter 22

A Prime Prerequisite

The Authorized or King James version, apparently because the translators were Catholics, mistranslated the following verses so they would appear to favor sacramentalism. Nearly all group-translated revisions have, strange to say, done likewise.

In Matt. 3:11 "I indeed baptize you with water unto (for in RSV and NIV) repentance." The preposition *eis* usually has the connotation of in, into or for, but *unto* is wrong. In the above verse, the word *for* does not fit the context, which definitely states that John the Baptist refused to baptize people who had not repented—"Bear fruit that is expressive (or proof) of repentance" (v.8). Josephus (*Antiq.* Bk. 19,5,2) confirms this interpretation that repentance was to precede baptism, by saying "John commanded the Jews to exercise virtue . . . and so to come to baptism, supposing the soul was thoroughly *purified beforehand* by righteousness."

Four articles appeared in 1951 and 1952 in the internationally read *Journal of Biblical Literature,* vols. 70 and 71, on *The Causal Use of Eis in the New Testament,* two by me and two by Dr. Ralph Marcus of the University of Chicago, who did not question its being used causally in the New Testament, but he questioned its causal use in nonbiblical passages that I cited, stating "It is quite possible that *eis* is used causally in these N.T.

105

passages." So the correct translation is, "I baptize you in (not with) water because of repentance."

The *Manual Grammar of the Greek New Testament,* pp. 103–4, which came off the press over fifty years ago, and *The Expositor* (London) 1923, did not carry sufficient weight with most translators apparently. They should have *studied Greek grammar.*

In Acts 2:47, "And the Lord added to the church daily such as *should be* saved" (AV). Both the RV and NIV rightly have "those who were being saved," which is correct. In Acts 2:38, "Repent and be baptized every one of you for the remission of sins." "For the forgiveness of sins" as in RSV and other versions is preferable. But more important is the command to repent before baptism, and the statement "you shall receive the gift of the Holy Spirit," implies that Luke meant that only born-again people were being baptized. That type of members profoundly and favorably impress their acquaintances.

The mistranslation, "wash away your sins," in Acts 22:16 implies that forgiveness of sins may be obtained by baptism. The ending of the verb *apolousai* (wash) is "middle," i.e., passive, not active, and the same as on the verb *baptisai.* So both verbs should be translated: "Be baptised and have your sins washed away by *calling* (instrumental use of the participle) on His name." This is wrongly translated in all group translations. Dr. C.B. Williams translated it correctly.

Chapter 23

You Said It

The idiomatic expressions, *su eipas, you said* (Matt. 26:64), and *su legeis, you say* (Matt. 15:2; Luke 22:70 and John 18:37) are translated in the regular versions (the R.S. included) literally as above, but nevertheless incorrectly, for Greek usage without and within the NT proves that they mean simply "yes" and are the equivalent of our slang expression "you said it."

In Xenophon's *Anabasis,* in the record of the trial of Orontas (I.6.7), in answer to a question, the statement follows: *ephe ho Orontas,* which means in the context, *yes.* In Matt. 26:64, we also have a trial scene. When Jesus was put on oath and asked if he were the Christ, he answered "you said," for which the parallel passage in Mark 14:62 has "I am." This fact in itself should have been sufficient evidence of the idomatic meaning of "you said." Goodspeed quotes Sophocles' *Oedipus the King,* 1475, as having a similar usage of *lego: "lego ti; legeis"* translated by Torr in the "Loeb Library," "Am I right? 'Tis true!"

Chapter 24

The Lord's Day (Rev. 1:10)

The only time the Lord's day, *kuriake hemera,* occurs in the New Testament is in Rev. 1:10, "I was in the Spirit on the Lord's day." Some, because of their theory that nearly all of Revelation depicts what will happen on earth in a seven-year period between the rapture and the second coming of Christ, interpret the Lord's day to mean here that John, the author, saw the future as the Lord did.

Unfortunately for such interpreters, there is nothing in this context to imply such a meaning; neither is there an example anywhere in the Bible to imply anything like that, and most damaging of all to such a theory is the fact that every occurrence of the expression in Christian literature indicates that it is a synonym for Sunday, as the following second-century quotations prove: "Having come together on the Lord's day, break bread and give thanks, having confessed your sins beforehand, in order that your sacrifice may be pure" (Didache). "On the day of the sun all in common come together, since it is the first day in which God, having changed the darkness and the matter, made a world, and Jesus Christ our Savior on that day arose from the dead. For they crucified him the day before Kronikos and on the day after Kronikos (Saturday), which is the day of the sun, having appeared to his apostles and disciples, he taught these things which we

108

submit to you for your consideration'' (Justin Martyr). ''No longer observing sabbaths, but fashioning their lives after the Lord's day'' (Ignatius, Magn. 9). ''The Lord's day began to dawn'' (Ev. Pet. ver 35). ''We keep the eighth day with gladness on which Jesus rose from the dead'' (Barn; 15:9). On ''the first day of the week,'' Christians observed the Lord's Supper (Acts 20:7), and gave money for the poor (1 Cor. 16:2).

Chapter 25

Inadequately Translated Words in the New Testament

The material in this paper is not so much philological as it is practical. In these castastrophic times, we seem to need more heart reinforcement than we do head enlightenment.

The Greek word *pistis,* meaning faith, is translated rightly in the R. S. V. in practically every instance. Out of twenty-four occurrences in the LXX, it connotes the idea of *faithfulness* or *trustworthiness* seventeen times, and means *faith* or *proof* only seven times. All these meanings are prevalent in koine Greek. In Matt. 23:23, it is properly rendered *faithfulness;* "justice, mercy, *faithfulness.*" Also in Rom. 3:3 and Gal. 5:23, "Their unfaithfulness did not annul the *faithfulness* of God, did it?" . . . "The fruit of the Spirit is," among other things, *"faithfulness* and self-control." But this idea of fidelity is a fundamental part of the word; and even where it is regularly translated *faith,* it also has besides the plus connotation of *faithfulness.* Thus, faith in God implies also faithfulness to God.

The word *akouo* is not translated to *heed* or *obey* in the N. T. as often as it could be. It is so used frequently in the LXX. Cf. Jer. 11:3, "Cursed be the man that will not obey the words of this covenant." When so translated, it helps to clarify what is expected in discipleship: John 5:24, "He that *heeds* my word

110

and believes him that sent me has eternal life"; John 8:47, "He that is of God *obeys* the words of God"; John 10:3, "The sheep *obey* his voice and he calls his own sheep by name"; John 10:27, "My sheep *obey* my voice and I know them." Jones revision of Liddell and Scott has these meanings for *akouo.*

Since the revised and R. S. version have corrected the mistranslation in the A. version of *apeitheo* in John 3:36, where it means *does not obey,* mention is merely made of it. However, correction helps to point out that saving faith seems to include readiness to obey Christ. The verse reads: "He that believes on the Son has eternal life; he that *does not obey* the Son shall not see life, but the wrath of God abides on him."

The basic meaning for the Greek word *diatheke* is *agreement.* It has this connotation thirty-one times in the N. T. to only two meaning a *will.*

That man's favor with God was conditioned by man's readiness to obey God is readily observable when one examines God's dealings with Israel. Abraham's good standing with God depended upon continuous obedience to God, as is recorded in Gen. 17:12 and 22:18: "Walk before me and be thou perfect. And I will make my covenant between me and thee. . . . In thy seed shall all the nations be blessed, because thou hast obeyed my voice."

In Exod. 19:7–8 we have the account of the institution of the covenant at Mt. Sinai. After Moses read to the Israelites what God's demands upon them would be, they ratified the covenant by saying, "All that Jehovah hath spoken we will do." Here God demanded and received a pledge of full obedience. Because this agreement was not kept by the people, they suffered the consequences of their disobedience in numerous ways until they were all eliminated, with the exception of Caleb and Joshua, who alone out of the whole multitude entered the promised land.

To retain God's favor, every generation was required to renew its covenant with God. God's blessings and protection were always conditioned by man's readiness to do God's will. Jeremiah (11:3) reminded the captive Israelites of his generation of this by saying, "Thus saith the Lord God of Israel: Cursed be the man that obeyeth not the words of this covenant.'' Emphasizing the same truth, Daniel (9:11) said: "All Israel have transgressed thy law, even by departing, so that they do not obey thy voice; therefore the curse is poured upon them.''

The New Testament answer to the question as to whether God requires less from His people today than He did then is that He requires more. Jesus' statement, "to whomsoever much shall be given of him shall also much be required,'' is sufficient proof of that. But by frequent and varied reiteration of teachings, dealing with the exacting nature of discipleship, Jesus informed would-be-followers that nothing less than willingness to do God's will, and continuous obedience to Him, would be acceptable with Him. The demands were too drastic for the rich young ruler and nearly all the rest that heard Jesus. The austere condition, "If anyone would come after me, let him deny himself and take up his cross daily, and let him continue following me'' (Luke 9:23), was too severe for most people, then, as well as now.

An untranslated meaning of the Greek word *omologeo,* which is regularly translated *confess* in the New Testament, throws considerable light on what Christ expected of His followers. In 127 contextual usages observed in koine Greek outside the New Testament, it was discovered to have the meaning of *agree* ninety-seven times, while it meant to *confess* only thirty times. It is very common in Greek papyri contracts, meaning to agree, as in P. Oxy II, No. 275, "Tryphon and Ptolemaeus *agree* with one another . . . Tryphon to apprentice his son to Thoonis for one year.'' Even when the context demands the translation *acknowledge* in the papyri in business documents, it refers to an agreement implied or specified. An example occurs in Cat. of Gk. P. No. 162, "She the *acknowledging (omologousa)* party, has, in accordance with this agreement *(omologian),* sold the half share of a house and yard.''

Although *omologeo* should regularly be translated to acknowledge or confess in practically every passage in the New Testament where it occurs, we still would do well to remember that the basic meaning is to agree and that the expression of acknowledgment or confession is rooted in and dependent upon an agreement either implied or made by the individual concerned. Or, in other words, the confession is supposed to spring from a genuine experience of decision to conform to the will of Christ or God. In all the papyri usages, even where the correct translation is *acknowledge,* the contexts always imply that an agreement, which is already in force or has already been made, is being acknowledged.

When we apply this meaning to the passages in the New Testament, we at once observe a richer content of meaning than was apparent before. Acts 7:17 may very appropriately be translated, "And as the time of the promise drew near which God had agreed *(omologesen)* with Abraham (reference to Gen. 17:1–2, where *diatheke* is used to mean agreement), the people grew and multiplied in Egypt." Matt. 10:32 has much more in it than most people are aware of. In that verse, Jesus said, "Everyone who shall *agree* with me *(omologesei en emoi)* before men, I will agree with him *(en auto)* before my Father who is in heaven." No attempt is even made in our English translations to translate the prepositional phrases *en emoi* (with me) and *en anto* (with him), and these prepositional phrases do not fit in with the word confess, but they do most appropriately with agree. (Was Jesus making a demand here, parallel to what God asked of the Israelites at Mount Sinai (Exod. 19:7–8)? After God's law was read to them, they responded, "All that Jehovah hath spoken we will do." There the demands of the old covenant were presented; here the primary condition of the new covenant, which is willingness to prove and to confess our faith in Christ by loyal and continuous obedience to him.) And certainly Jesus required nothing less than a readiness to agree with him when he demanded full obedience to God, as recorded in Matt. 7:21, "Not everyone that says to me Lord, Lord, shall enter into the Kingdom of heaven, but he that does the will of my Father in heaven."

When Paul in Rom. 10:9 says, "Because if thou shalt confess with thy mouth Jesus as Lord," he evidently meant, if we consider the basic meaning of the verb and its prevalent usage during his century, that nothing short of a willingness to agree to make Christ Lord of one's life would suffice to obtain salvation.

For the word implies that one speaks the same things that another does, or that he enters into an agreement with him.

So to confess one's sins implies then that the worshiper takes the same attitude toward sin that God does, that he profess to look at sin from God's viewpoint, and that he determines or agrees to live as God expects of him. To confess Jesus as Savior means that one agrees with him, taking his attitude toward God, men, sin, service, righteousness, life, etc.

A splendid and suggestive statement of what confessing Christ meant in the early part of the second century A.D. is found in 2 Clement, Sec. 3–4:

> But by means of what do we confess him? By doing what he says, and by not disobeying his commandments and by not honoring him with our lips only but with all the heart and all the mind. So then, brethren, let us *confess* him by means of our deeds, by loving one another, not by being jealous, but by exercising self-control, by being merciful and good, and we ought to sympathize with each other, and not to be lovers of money. By these deeds we confess him and not by the opposite kind.

The author of Hebrews declares that Jeremiah's prophecy (31:31), that God would make a new covenant and put his laws into people's minds and write them upon their hearts, was fulfilled in the coming of Christ, and he calls him the mediator of a better covenant (8:6–10). Since the word covenant primarily means an agreement, it is naturally a matter of deep interest to discover what Christ offers to do and also what he expects of us in this agreement. In instituting the Lord's Supper, Jesus called the fruit of the grape "my blood of the covenant" and stated what his part of the covenant, or agreement, implied by saying, "which is poured out for the many (i.e., for all who would become his disciples) for the forgiveness of sins."

To share in this forgiveness, man is expected to enter into a covenant with Jesus, agreeing to accept him as Savior (John 1:12; 5:24; 14:6; Acts 4:12), repent of his sins (Mark 1:5; Luke

13:3; Acts 2:38; 3:19; 17:30), and become a lifelong servant of Christ, seeking to obey him in every area of his life, and emulating him in character and service (John 3:36; Acts 5:29,32; Rom. 6:16). "He is the author of salvation" only "to those that obey him," according to the writer of Hebrews (5:9).

If in presenting Christ's claims, we set forth only the necessity of faith in Christ for the present, and repentance of sins for the past, and stop there, and fail to preach the rest of the gospel, which for the future demands lifetime obedience to Christ and continuous service to men, do we not misrepresent Christ and emasculate his Gospel and do we not actually prevent people from finding entrance into his Kingdom? James said "faith without works is dead," and Christ said, "By their fruits you shall know them." When Christ invited people to become his followers, he stressed the cost to them in personal self-sacrifice and demanded discipline and lifetime service, motivated by love and a spirit of humility. Is this not what he meant when he said, "Except a grain of wheat fall into the earth and die it abides by itself alone." . . . "If you love me you *will* keep my commandments"?

One of the most difficult questions we face is what is to be the fate of those Christians who have relapsed. Ezekiel (33:13,18) states positively that such people have forfeited their standing with God. "When the righteous turns from his righteousness, and commits iniquity, he shall even die thereby." The New Testament does teach that forgiveness for occasional acts of sin follows repentance. Peter was forgiven after he repented for having denied Christ, and John said, "If any man commits an act of sin, we have an advocate with the Father." But John also made clear that the so-called Christian, or anyone else, who continues sinning was beyond the pale of God's mercy by saying, "He that goes on sinning belongs to the Devil" (1 John 3:8). Jesus seems to have taught the same when he said, "No man who puts his hand to the plow and looks back is fit for the kingdom of God" (Luke 9:62). He certainly implied that one must continue being loyal to Christ by saying, "He that endures to the end shall be saved" (Matt. 10:22). Certainly, theological consistency should not encourage Christians to become guilty of spiritual inactivity or of any other sin.

The most important command, Jesus said, was to love God. John defines this to consist in obeying God: 1 John 5:3, "This is the love of God that we keep his commandments." He bluntly affirms that anyone who claims to be a Christian and does not obey God "is a liar and the truth is not in him" (1 John 2:4).

But it is in Hebrews that the warning of tragic and eternal consequences for continued disobedience and disloyalty is stated most bluntly and clearly in the New Testament. The author says "it is impossible to restore again to repentance those who have once been enlightened" and who go on, by their conduct, showing disrespect for Christ (6:4–6). The same writer taught that sinning willfully is certain to meet with eternal punishment, and he says, "How much worse punishment do you think will be deserved by the man who has spurned the Son of God, and desecrated the blood of the covenant by which he was consecrated, and has disgraced the Spirit of grace" (10:26–29)?

We conclude this study with the warning that Jesus gave in his conclusion to the Sermon on the Mount. After saying "Not everyone who says to me, Lord, Lord, shall enter into the kingdom of heaven, but he that practices doing (force of the Greek present participle) the will of my Father," he went on to say, "Everyone who heeds these words and puts them into practice shall be likened to a wise man who built his house upon rock. . . . But everyone who does not heed these words and does not practice them shall be likened to a foolish man who built his house upon sand . . . and it fell and its fall was great. (Matt. 7:21, 24–27).[1]

Note

1. (This paper was read January 13, 1951, at the meeting of the *National Association of Biblical Instructors,* University of Chicago.)

Chapter 26

Youth's Greatest Problem

Youth's greatest weakness is the readiness to follow the crowd. A high school boy has written, "My greatest trouble is learning to say 'No' to the crowd." A high school girl states the same fact thus, "A girl's biggest temptation is to be a good sport when out with a crowd and to do what the crowd does."

The following experiences, which were written anonymously and describe the writers' greatest temptations, show how grave and how prevalent this temptation is.

A Tennessee University Lad

A great problem that confronted me that I had to face, happened about a year ago. The boys I ran with all played pool, and drank and gambled. They tried to influence me that way. And I did take part in it for a while but one day I began to look at my future and the first thing a man would ask if he wanted to employ me was if I drank and about my character. But still I kept drifting on, going to dances, drinking, and going to indecent places. And then *I changed associates*. It was hard at first to quit the old gang, when they would ask me to go out with them. But I soon broke away. I feel lots better since I quit those things and I do not think they will pay in the long run. I think your future depends upon your young life, how it is spent. It was much easier to go in the old way, but does it pay in the future? That was the question I asked myself. So I am living a clean life now.

A Chicago High School Girl

Plans had been made for a good time that sounded more like a rough-neck riot than anything else. Another girl was needed and the problem was put up to me. The glamour of it as painted by my friends, tempted me to a great extent. Dancing and dining soon had my mind in a whirl. Naturally I thought about this party for days to come, the more I thought about it the less I wanted to go. The glitter grew duller, and there finally crept into my mind the suspicion that probably this party had a preference for cabarets and petting. I met the folks of the party, and from all appearances they appeared to be swell. The longer they knew you the coarser they became. I decided that I'd go anyway. One must be initiated into the arts of cabareting and petting; so I thought then. I got all set, and the day before, my conscience bothered me. Things my parents had told me came to my mind. "Never become cheap even in the eyes of your cheapest friends." "Hold your conscience above the mire of low-minded people." "Always be sweet, unsoiled by others, save yourself for a real love." At the last minute I decided to back out. I was called "baby," "innocent," "Mama's girl." But I'd sooner be that than a "cheap sport," and as for "mama's girl" and "innocent," I love my mother and father; I think they're perfect, and somehow they are always right. I would sooner listen to them than all the gay young fluttering people, who think they are having a good time. I have never regretted my refusal. As for happiness, the right kind of folks, a good home, and a clear conscience would always keep one happy.

A New Mexico College Girl

About a year ago, I was with a group of young people with whom I had not associated in their parties as my parents did not approve of their friendship. This time I happened to be with their crowd. Being the only new one in their gang or set, I was of course supposed to follow in what they did "like a good sport," and "have a good time like the rest." When I did not I was laughed at and made fun of. It was embarrassing and humiliating beyond words—standing alone against the group. I was tempted and thought "what harm can it be?" The other girls in the group petted, drank and smoked. When offered a drink I raised the bottle to my lips. At this time the thought of my parents came to me—their sorrow at knowing that I would do this. Then I knew it was wrong, that it could not do me any good, but would do much harm. I did not, and I have the friendship of these boys and girls and also their respect.

Young people are often accused of not being good sports when they refuse to enter into whatever the person or group of persons proposes. If a group is drinking, stealing, or going to a house of ill-fame and one does not care to join them, he is dubbed a poor sport or a "flat tire." Or, regardless of what a crowd is doing, be it ever so indecent, if one, because of higher ideals, refuses to do as the rest, he is likely to be called a poor sport. That being true, it is not at all complimentary to be called a good sport. For its usage suggests that a good sport is one who conforms to whatever others do. As long as no evil is proposed, it is, of course, best in most cases to conform, but when conformity means compromise with principles, then it is best to be a poor sport and to display enough backbone and spunk to discourage further ridicule on the part of the offenders. God gave people tempers and wills to use for just such occasions.

119

A South Carolina University Lad

Two summers ago, while working on a boat in Charleston I had a great temptation. One evening about eight o'clock, after we had finished a hard day's work the crew decided to take a couple of drinks.

I had been a member of the church for about two years and I was trying to live right. The boys offered me a drink but I refused. Then they began to make fun of me, they called me "mamma's boy" and everything but what a man should be. I wanted to be a man and no "sissy." I thought it was a disgrace to be called a sissy, so I decided to take a drink. But just as I put the bottle to my mouth I came to and saved myself and asked myself what would my mother think if she knew I took a drink. I knew it would break her heart and probably send her to an early grave. I thought of what the people of my community would think and say and above all, my Lord—what would he think? Then I said "No, I won't take a drink." I prefer to be a "sissy" before these men rather than to be an outcast before my people and my Lord who died for my sins. I was almost persuaded, but by the help of the Lord Jesus Christ I was able to overcome the temptation. We can all overcome temptation if we will just stop and think before we act.

An Indiana High School Lad

One Sunday night I was in Sellersburg with some boys of my age and my schoolmates when some one mentioned going "out for a big time." I wanted to go and they wanted me to take them, as I was the only one of the crowd that owned a car. I had come to town with the intention of attending church, which I knew was the proper thing to do. St. Joe was to be our first stop, a noted place for purchasing whiskey,

120

moonshine or anything along such lines. They promised to buy gasoline, all the drinks and pay all other expenses. I refused to go, and they teased me about being a coward and yellow. I wanted to go, yet I know that it wasn't right. They begged me, but I turned and walked off towards church with slurs and boos ringing in my ears.

A South Carolina University Boy

Last year a problem confronted me as a Freshman. It was what fraternity to join. At ――――― there are three national fraternities and several locals. I was being rushed by one of the best nationals and what I believe to be the last local. The idea of wearing a real fraternity pin and being a real fraternity man greatly appealed to me. In fact, it almost closed my eyes to numerous other factors that should not be overlooked. What kind of boys were there in each club? Here was really the important question. These were going to be the fellows with whom I was to live for four years. Were they my type and were they boys whom I could love as brothers? I asked myself these questions over and over and pondered the matter for a long time. The fellows in the national fraternity (as I gradually found out) drank and gambled a lot. They thought nothing of running around with crooked women. As far as I knew (and as I afterward found to be true) the boys in the local were all nice fellows, more my type. Thus, I was pulled between two factors, a fraternity pin and a good bunch of boys. I do not know exactly why I decided as I did. Perhaps it was my early training at home, the thought of what my mother would want me to do. At any rate, I went local and never regretted it. In fact, every day I am more thoroughly convinced that I did the right thing.

Courage, a Rare Virtue

It has been said that the most fundamental virtue is moral courage. At any rate, it is altogether too rare in most people's lives. All of us are inclined to be cowards in a crowd if we are in danger of being laughed at and ridiculed. Character can be acquired and maintained only to the degree that we put convictions and principles before crowds in our scheme of values. Ibsen, the great Norwegian dramatist, wrote, "The strongest man is the man that stands alone."

Christ or the Crowd?

The masses have always lived on a low, animal plane. Only a minority have had the grit and the courage to live as human beings, endowed with a soul that must "give an account to God for every deed done in the flesh," ought to live. For a while, great crowds thronged Jesus and even assayed to make him king. But, when He made clear to them His mission was primarily to reconcile people with God rather than to inaugurate an earthly, utopian regime, the crowd deserted him. So it has been ever since. People prefer the temporal instead of the eternal, the present instead of the future, the material instead of the spiritual. They want to satisfy the appetites of the body rather than the desires of the soul. Only a few rise above the level of the common herd. These believe that they are more than animals, that they have immortal souls, and that the most important accomplishment of man is to live in conformity with the will of God.

The apostle John relates how on a certain occasion the crowds deserted Jesus and how Jesus asked his disciples to choose whether they would follow him or the crowd. "Simon Peter answered him, Lord, to whom shall we go? Thou hast the words of eternal life. And we have believed and know that thou art the Holy One of God" (John 6:68–69). Jesus had said, "if any man would come after me let him deny himself and let him take up his cross daily and follow me" (Luke 9:23). In other words, one must choose whether he will follow Christ or the crowd. It is easy to follow the crowd, but difficult to follow Christ. But "he that obeyeth not the Son shall not see life for the wrath of God abideth on him" (John 3:36). To follow him is the only way to find peace and pardon. "Who follows in his train?" It takes courage to be a Christian.

> Dare to do right. Dare to be true.
> Other men's failures can never save you.
> Stand by your conscience, your honor, your faith.
> Stand like a hero and battle till death.

Chapter 27

"God in the Cheese Business"

A young man, twenty-one years old, came to Chicago with the ambition of building up a big business. His capital consisted of but sixty-five dollars. For three years, he toiled unceasingly against overwhelming and insurmountable odds. He was hopelessly in debt. He had failed. He had given himself but one more day to decide whether he should abandon his business. The crisis was at hand.

At the close of that day, he was throughly convinced that he was a failure. He was asking himself why he had failed. As Paul of old, he was startled to hear an invisible speaker's voice, for he heard to his astonishment the words, "You have not had God in your business." He considered it a message from God and pondered it as such. After a few moments of heart-searching deliberation, he heard himself saying, "If God wants to run the cheese business, he can run it." From that time on, he has considered God the main partner of the firm.

The man who had that experience is Mr. J. L. Kraft, of the cheese company that has the reputation of being the biggest cheese concern in the world. He is a deacon of the North Shore Baptist church in Chicago, and is also superintendent of its Sunday school. He began his work in denominational activities, outside his church, by becoming a trustee of the Northern Baptist Theological Seminary. He is chairman of its investment committee and, in that capacity, renders valuable service, as well as by his frequent and generous gifts. He is also president of the Chicago Baptist Social Union.

Mr. Kraft has boundless faith in God's readiness to answer prayer and is fervent in his passion to serve him. Two anecdotes out of his life help one to understand what type of man he is.

A car that he and one of his brothers were riding in turned over and pinned him underneath. A large part of the weight of the car was resting on his chest, and he was gradually dying from suffocation. His brother tried to lift the car, but was unable. There was nothing around that could be used as a pry. No one was in sight to help, and death seemed imminent. The stricken and dying man realized the seriousness and the hopelessness of his predicament. It seemed useless to pray, but he felt impressed to do so, so he did. Then he lapsed into unconsciousness. When he became conscious again, his brother was calling to him and telling him to move backward. By doing so, he extricated himself. Upon being asked, his brother explained that in desperation he had lifted the car, in spite of the fact that it weighed over a ton. Consequently, Mr. Kraft firmly believes that God helped his brother lift that car. Such experiences as this have caused him to have implicit faith in prayer.

A few years ago, Mr. Kraft was scheduled to address two hundred salesmen, mostly of his company, from all parts of the United States. He felt impressed to talk to them on the importance of being a Christian, but his judgment argued that such a talk would be out of place at a business convention. Rather, he should talk about promoting business and try to arouse these men to greater enthusiasm for selling Kraft cheese. So he prepared a speech of the latter type. However, the first impression still clung tenaciously to him, so much so that when the occasion came, he actually abandoned his prepared speech and instead urged upon the men the prime importance of following Christ. It was most unusual, and it was certainly the unconventional thing to do. But God greatly blessed that response to his leadership, for about 75 percent of those men have personally informed Mr. Kraft since

125

that time how much that talk helped them, and many of them were influenced by it to become Christians. As a result of it, a few weeks ago, a salesman surrendered to Chirst in a mission in Texas and wrote Mr. Kraft a "thank-you" letter.

He does not hestiate to speak to a man about Christ if he believes there is a chance to help the man, whether it is in his office or in church. His wife has the same readiness to serve, and both are exceedingly effective in soul winning. But why should not all Christians have such a habit? Was not this the New Testament way?

It is also of interest to know that he believes it pays to give liberally to further Christianity. He began by giving a tithe, but he does not think that enough, so he now gives considerably more. He gives not to make more money, but to do good. But from experience, he has learned that God never fails to reward liberality. A striking fact in favor of his viewpoint is that with scarcely an exception, he says, every big business concern in the United States has an active Christian at the head of it.

Mr. Kraft does not know that these things are being written about him. Because it helped the writer to know that a hard-headed, shrewd businessman finds it practical, profitable, and pleasureable to treat God as a partner, he is writing this, trusting that others will also be inspired by this man's devotion.

More men each year are assuming a biblical basis for business. They are finding Jesus' teaching to be practicable in business as well as in every other phase of life. Is it not strange that men call him Lord and yet go on treating his teachings as if impracticable? If God made this cheese business succeed, will he not make any other legitimate businesses succeed, providing he is allowed a voice in its control and a fair percentage of its profits?

Personality Builders

Dr. L. R. Hogan, professor of education at Union University, says that when several years ago, he was debating whether to stay in the teaching profession, it was the realization that he was actually and visibly building personalities that caused him to continue teaching. The teacher has more young people in his classes than the minister has in the congregation, normally, and he has contact with them five days per week to the minister's one, so that he has, because of the regularity of his contact, incomparable possibilities for molding and shaping young lives.

The high esteem with which pupils regard their teachers makes teaching a mighty power in character building as well as a source of unceasing joy. Many children are helped more by their teachers than they are by their parents. The child's first view of real life comes in the schoolroom. To the extent that the teacher is kind, sympathetic, and capable, to that extent will he be loved and followed. Young minds, after all, are the only minds that can be shaped and guided. Old minds are enslaved in ruts of thought and are incapable of changing much. Those expressions of appreciation, whether a compliment, an apple, or a gift from a class, which comes occasionally, are rays of joy that penetrate and delight the teacher's heart. Then, as the pupils grow up and assume worthy tasks in life, who would object to the teacher claiming credit, at least in part, for his pupils' success?

Chapter 28

Revelation or the Apocalypse

Introduction

Alexander Ramsey opens his discussion on this book, in the *Westminster New Testament*, with these significant words: "If we are to understand the Revelation or Apocalypse, we must bear in mind that it arose out of the circumstances of the church in its author's day and was addressed to his own generation. All attempts to find in its bizarre imagery of the fortunes of the church to the end of time, or a forecast of the history of the world in coming centuries, are foredoomed to failure. That way confusion lies." The author of the Apocalypse, who we believe was the apostle John, the son of Zebedee, very specifically stated that the events he describes were transpiring at that time or immediately thereafter: "Which it is necessary to happen quickly . . . for the time is near . . . which must shortly come to pass . . . the time is near" (1:1,3:22:6,10).

In view of these clues, given by the author himself, and since sound exegesis approaches all the other NT books by interpreting them in the light of the people and situations prevalent at the time of writing, the same method should be followed in studying the Apocalypse (*apocalupsis-uncovering*. Practically all commentaries on the book written within the past half century have done this, C.F. Swete, William and *Alex* Ramsey, Charles Beckwith, Moffatt, A.T. Robertson, W.T. Conner, H.E. Dana. Robertson says: John was writing about Rome. . . . He wanted to cheer them and I think he wrote to cheer us with a picture not of history, but of a world struggle between Christianity and the devil. . . . Harnack says it is the plainest book in the NT. On the other hand, South says it either finds a man mad or makes him mad. . . . It is the most abused book in the NT, made to mean anything or nothing." Irenaeus (A.D. 170) has informed us that John was writing during Domitian's reign. (A.D. 81–96) and that the situation he describes was prevalent then: "uttered by him. Who saw the apocalypse. For it was seen no such long time ago, almost in our own generation, at the end of the reign of Dometian."

Historical Background

The Christians in Asia Minor near the close of the first century needed encouragement, guidance, and authoritative apostolic teachings. While there were heresies to combat then, as there have been in every generation since then, John, though touching on these, in the seven letters, was burdened primarily because of Domitian's self-proclamation that he was a god and his demand that he be worshiped as such. This created the most critical crisis Christianity faced in that generation. To comply was impossible. To resist meant certain death for many. John had been arrested and exiled to Patmos (an island nearby in the Aegean sea, about ten by six miles in size). Whatever John wrote was doubtless subject to censorship, so he could not get a letter through in which resistance to Rome was encouraged openly. How? By using apocalypic imagery, which was in general usage among Jews and Christians and very likely fairly well understood, he managed to outwit his Roman guards, who couldn't understand, and at the same time, succeeded in giving vital and martyr-making information to the sorely troubled Christians of his day.

Antiochus Epiphanes (170–160 B.C.) had sought to exterminate Judaism and to substitute polytheism during his reign in Syria. He had defiled the temple and had it rededicated to a pagan god. He required monthly pagan sacrifices, proscribed circumcision, Sabbath keeping, and Bible reading. But *the Jews* under the Maccabeans staged a successful but bloody revolt, and after years of terrific struggle, won first religious, and later on, 100 years of independence. They became subject in 63 B.C., through the invasion of Pompey, to Rome, which as a whole was tolerant toward their religion. However, in A.D. 40, Cajus Caligula, depraved and partly demented, sought to have a statue of himself put into the temple in Jerusalem, to be worshiped as a god. The Jews rose up almost to a man in protest against such and Petronius, the governor of Syria, with great difficulty and after considerable delay, succeeded in getting the decree rescinded. But the emperor was so peeved over it that he ordered Petronious to commit suicide. But Caligula's death soon after made the order ineffective. Philo went from Alexandria with a delegation to Rome to protest Caligula's demand on the Jews, but he and those with him were insolently treated. The Jews in this crisis preferred to lose their fortunes and even their lives rather than to be disloyal to their God.

In 64 A.D., Rome, in the reign of Nero, had a devastating fire. Nero was blamed for it by the populace. Looking for a scapegoat, he accused the Christians of being guilty. No one knows how many hundreds were tortured and slain as a result of the emperor and his government turning against them with this mad and moblike slaughter. Possibly both Paul and Peter lost their lives as a result of this defenseless decision by Nero. Although this persecution seems to have been limited chiefly to the city of Rome, it nevertheless resulted in dire consequences for Christians all over the empire, because it meant that Christianity was an illegal religion, so much so that anyone professing to belong to it could legally be condemned to death. Up to this time, Christians had been protected because of their Jewish connection. Fortunately, few judges enforced Nero's decree against them.

But when Domitian became emperor, he decreed that his subjects were to worship him as a god. The Christians naturally refused to do this. They were in immediate danger of being dealt with as if guilty of capital crimes and were subject to capital punishment. Mommsen says: "The persecution of Christians was a standing matter, as was that of robbers. All calamities were blamed on the Christians. Domitian had himself called our Lord and our God." He was so determined to receive such adulation and worship that he had his own cousin Flourius Clemens put to death and his wife, Domitilla, exiled to an island because they refused to comply. The people of the province of Asia were most responsive to the emperor's wishes because, after a recent damaging earthquake, they had been generously helped from the emperor's treasury. So they readily had his image put in temples in their area and even built temples in his honor in Pergamum, Ebhesus, and Smyrna, cities to which John addressed specific letters. On specific days, possibly once a month, every resident was expected to worship before Domitian's image. Those who refused were subject to persecution. Their choice had to be either to worship Lord Domitian or the Lord Jesus. But if they decided to remain loyal to the latter, their standing, property, and lives were in jeopardy. John urged them to die rather than to compromise.

Apocalyptic Literature

The singular type of a symbolism found in the Apocalypse had been in frequent use by the Jews for centuries. Ezekiel and Daniel are the earliest examples. The former set forth his visions of the dry bones, the future temple, the river flowing from the temple, and of the wheels within wheels. The latter graphically depicted four beasts to represent four kingdoms (Chapters 7–8), and he used the number seven and multiples and fractions of its seventy weeks . . . seven weeks . . . one week, and also used several expressions and pictures about the Messiah, which are used in a similar manner in the Apocalypse.

In books of this type, which flourished especially when Judaism was a subject nation and when the hand of the oppressor was heavy on it, information was conveyed through the use of visions, which the writers claimed they had while in a trance or in high moments of spiritual ecstasy. Bizarre imagery of weird fantastic animals, or of scenes beyond human experience on earth, or beyond what had ever been seen before in the heavens above, depict symbolically certain ideas the author was trying to make others understand. Truth is portrayed through the medium of pen pictures, somewhat as is being done today through cartoons. Each picture is a symbol for a truth suggested by the picture. Or, information is conveyed by indirect language. The method was somewhat like the use of allegories, but differed especially in that weird, unnatural symbols or pictures were used in apocalyptic literature.

Noncanonical books of this type are: Enoch (170–65 B.C.), Testament of the Twelve Patriarchs (135–105 B.C.), Apocalypse of Moses (135–105 B.C.); Psalter of Solomon (70–45 B.C.), Secrets of Enoch (first century A.D.), Assumption of Moses (A.D. 10), Apocalypse of Baruch (A.D. 50–90), Apocalypse of Ezra or 2 Esdras (A.D. 81–96).

The first was written during Antiochus' brutal and unparalleled attempt to exterminate Jewish religion. The last seems to stem from Domitian's similar purpose, to wipe out Christianity. The main object of the authors was to console the persecuted and to encourage them to choose death rather than disloyalty to God or Christ. They pictured hope and certain victory in the near future, or at the coming of the Messiah, and most vividly and perfectly beyond death. They visualized great rewards awaiting the faithful; and inevitable and eternal punishment for their persecutors. These events are dealt with as in drama. Often God and his angels are in deadly combat with the devil and his demons. All kinds of calamaties befall the righteous, but only for a limited period of time, and then God intervenes in behalf of his own.

The book of Revelation views life, and pictures triumph over present afflictions from this viewpoint. It uses the same type of symbols and images that were used by Ezekiel, but more especially by Daniel and other apocalyptists. Truth is conveyed by way of drama, by a series of images, many arranged in groups of seven. Thus, to understand the message, we need to ascertain what the form signifies as to inner truth. To try to interpret each statement or picture literally is to ignore both the language that typifies the book and also the message that it represents. There is unquestionably prediction in it; persecution is short-lived, judgment awaits the wicked, rewards await the righteous in heaven, and Christ is coming to receive his own and to triumph ultimately and finally over all opposition. But we are not informed when he will make this triumphal entry upon the earth.

The main theme of the book is to promote loyalty to Christ in spite of human pressure to disown him. Thus, the ordinary aim of the author was practical, to defend and to extend Christ's reign. But drama is the vehicle used to accomplish this noble end. Following a scene in which men are being tortured because of their faith, over and over again, we find one in which they are rejoicing in heaven and being praised for their exceptional courage and fidelity while on earth. A few individuals will lose their lives in the struggle, but the cause is bound to triumph, and the individuals will be all the richer in eternity, to the extent that they served and suffer for Christ. Although the book was written, we believe, to help Christians in the Domicianic persecutions, nevertheless, it has the most pertinent and helpful message of the whole Bible for people, as in past generations so in ours, when they are undergoing persecution. Recent examples are the Christians in Korea and Russia. At such times, it gives unequaled help and courage to all oppressed Christians. No wonder, for it was written to meet just such a need.

However, failure to interpret this book as apocalyptic literature means to fail to understand it historically in its peculiar setting of persecution, means to fail to grasp its central and dominant message, and means consequently an unscholarly and an unsound interpretation of it. Not to study the book in its setting and not to realize its use of a type of language, (apocalypticism), which is alien to our experience, is to be at sea at understanding it. How can one understand the significance, for example, of the twelfth chapter, which pictures a woman (not a man), arrayed with the sun and the moon under her feet, and upon her head a crown of twelve stars; and she was with child, unless one realizes that the author is here using cosmological drama to picture how heaven helps those "that keep the commandments of God and hold to the testimony of Jesus"? The child "Who is to rule all the nations and was caught up" to God represents Christ, and "the rest of her seed" evidently represents believers in Christ. Although the dragon, who represents the Devil, can with one flip of his tail throw down one-third of all the stars in the heavens, he is nevertheless powerless in his attempts to conquer either the woman or her seed. What graphic, stupendous use of drama, so huge that all the universe is involved, and yet how consoling to Christians when under persecution!

Chapter 29

Jehovah's Witnesses

Dr. Julius R. Mantey
414 Palmetto Road
New Port Richey, Fla. 33552

Dear Brother Mantey:

Joan and I are so happy to have received your recent letter and to know that you are still active in His service helping people step from death to life. We are also busy speaking in many churches exposing the diabolical deceivers at the Watchtower headquarters.

Dr. Mantey, Joan and I were born in the Jehovah's Witness cult. Our parents are still JW's. We pray for them daily. I worked at the Watchtower Headquarters from 1950 to 1958. In 1951 and 1952 I worked in the "service department." I was responsible for answering Bible questions for ⅓ of the United States for JW's. I ate breakfast, dinner, and supper with these so-called Bible translators. None of them graduated from any college. In the book I helped write: *We Left Jehovah's Witnesses—a Nonprophet Organization* on p. 74 is this statement. "From my observation, N. H. Knorr, F. W. Franz, A.

D. Schroeder, G. D. Gangas, and M. Henschel met together in these translation sessions.''

Nathan Homer Knorr is the late president of JW's. He graduated from Allentown, Pa. high school. Had no knowledge of Greek or Hebrew and took no course in any Bible language. He, upon finishing high school, went to work as a shipping clerk at the Watchtower.

Fred William Franz is now President of Jehovah's Witnesses. He is really their Pope. He creates the theology of JW'S. All final answers to questions go to F W Franz not Knorr. Franz is responsible for the *New World Translation*. He claims to be a scholar. He attended the University of Cincinnati for 2 years. Quit in his sophomore year and Franz is sophomoric. He quit school in 1914 because the world was going to end that year. He had no formal study of Bible languages. He is a do-it-yourselfer in Hebrew.

Albert Darger Schroeder is the Registrar of the Watchtower school for missionaries. He had no training in Bible languages.

George Demetrius Gangas was born in Athens, Greece. He had no schooling. His qualification for being a Bible translator was being born in Athens. His picture is in the book *We Left Jehovah's Witnesses,* p. 69.

Milton George Henschel is now Vice President of JW'S. He grew up as a JW. I am not sure that he even graduated from high school. I am certain he never attended any college. He, I suspect, will be the new President of JW's.

Here then are the translators of the worst book ever printed on earth. They are diabolical deceivers. It is no wonder to me that they wish to remain anonymous. God bless you, Dr. Mantey.

Your brother in Christ
William I. Cetnar

The men whom Mr. Cetnar named in his letter were not qualified to translate the Bible or the New Testament. I have never read any New Testament so badly translated as *The Kingdom Interlinear Translation of the Greek Scriptures.* In fact, it is not their translation at all. Rather, it is a distortion of the New Testament.

The translators used what J. B. Rotherham had translated in 1893, in modern speech, and changed the readings in scores of passages to state what Jehovah's Witnesses believe and teach. That is *distortion,* not translation.

In their Foreword, page 7, is this shocking statement: ''No translation of these sacred writings into another language is inspired.''

By their own statement, they have admitted that theirs is not inspired. Certainly, all those passages they have distorted are not inspired because they teach the opposite of what is in the inspired Greek New Testament, the opposite of what Jesus and the apostles said and wrote. That is heresy of the rankest kind.

A Distorted Translation

It was in response to the question, ''Who do you claim to be?'' (John 8:53–58) that Jesus replied, ''Before Abraham I am'' (*ego eimi* in Greek). The translation of it as ''I have been'' by Jehovah's Witnesses is wrong. The footnote stating that it is in ''the perfect indefinite tense'' is also wrong. No Greek grammar, to my knowledge, has such a statement. In fact, there is no form of *eimi* in the perfect tense in the Greek New Testament.

Apparently, the mistranslation ''I have been'' was deliberately and diabolically used to deceive people. The mistranslators did not want people to know that ''God was in Christ reconciling the world to himself,'' which the apostle Paul stated in (2 Cor. 5:19), and as all NT versions have stated. Jesus said, ''If you do not believe that I am he (the Messiah) you will die in your sins'' (John 8:24). That means that all unbelievers are lost.

When Jesus said, ''Before Abraham I am'' (*ego eimi)* he was apparently quoting Exod. 3:14. ''Say to the people of Israel

I am *(ego eimi)* has sent me to you." In the next verse is the statement that "I am" meant "the-Lord, the God of your Fathers."

The fact that when Jesus said, "Before Abraham I am," the hearers picked up stones to throw at him, indicates that they thought he was guilty of blasphemy by his claiming to be God in human flesh. Jews did likewise when he said, "I and the Father are one" (John 10:31). When the high priest asked Jesus "Are you the Christ the Son of the Blessed?" Jesus said, "I am" *(ego eimi)* (Mark 14:62).

Similar evidence that Christ is exalted to the highest heights in Scripture is that both he and God are called "rock, *petra.*" God is so addressed in Pss. 19:14; 31:02; 62:02, and elsewhere.

Christ is so likened in 1 Cor. 10:04. "They drank from the spiritual rock *(petra)* that followed them." It is another of the scores of statements in the Bible affirming that, "Christ is our great God and Savior" (Titus 2:13).

A Grossly Misleading Translation

John 1:1, which reads "In the beginning was the Word and the Word was with God and the Word was God" is shockingly mistranslated, "Originally the Word was, and the Word was with God, and the Word was a god," in a *New World Translation of the Christian Greek Scriptures,* published under the auspices of Jehovah's Witnesses.

Since my name is used and our *Manual Grammar of the Greek New Testament* is quoted on page 744 to seek to justify their translation, I am making this statement.

The translation suggested in our grammar for the disputed passage is, "the Word was deity." Moffat's rendering is "the Word was divine." Williams's translation is, "the Word was God Himself." Each translation reflects the dominant idea in the Greek. For, whenever an article does not precede a noun in Greek, that noun can either be considered as emphasizing the character, nature, essence, or quality of a person or thing, as

138

theos (God) does in John 1:1, or it can be translated in certain contexts as indefinite, as they have done. But of all the scholars in the world, as far as we know, none have translated this verse as Jehovah's Witnesses have done.

If the Greek article occurred with both Word and God in John 1:1, the implication would be that they are one and the same person, absolutely identical. But John affirmed that "the Word was with (the) God" (the definite article preceding each noun), and in so writing, he indicated his belief that they are distinct and separate personalities. Then John next stated that the Word was God, i.e., of the same family or essence that characterizes the Creator. Or, in other words, that both are of the same nature, and that nature is the highest in existence, namely divine.

Examples where the noun in the predicate does not have an article, as in the above verse, are: John 4:24, "God is spirit," John 4:8, "God is love," Matthew 13:39, "the reapers are angels," i.e., they are the type of beings known as angels. In each instance, the noun in the predicate was used to describe some quality or characteristic of the subject, whether as to nature or type.

The apostle John, in the context of the introduction to his Gospel, is pulling all the stops out of language to portray not only the deity of Christ, but also his equality with the Father. He states that the Word was in the beginning, that He was *with* God, that He *was* God and that *all creation* came into existence through Him and that not even one thing exists that was not created by Christ. What else could be said that John did not say? In John 1:18, he explained that Christ has been so intimate with the Father that He was in His bosom and that He came to earth to exhibit or portray God. But if we had no other statement from John except that which is found in John 14:9, "He that has seen me has seen the Father," that would be enough to satisfy the seeking soul that Christ and God are the same in essence and that both are divine and equal in nature.

Besides, the whole tenor of New Testament revelation points in this direction. Compare Paul's declaration in Col. 1:19, for instance: "that all the divine fullness should dwell in Him," or

139

the statement in Hebrews, "He is the reflection of God's glory and the perfect representation of His being, and continues to uphold all the universe by His mighty word." (William's translation.) Note the sweeping, cosmic claim recorded in Matt. 28:19, "*All authority* has been given to me in heaven and on earth." In Phil. 2:5,9, "Who being in very nature *God . . .*God *exalted* him to the highest place and gave him the name that is *above* every name . . . and every tongue confess that Jesus Christ is Lord." In Col. 2:9–10, "For *In Christ* all the fullness of the Deity lives in bodily form . . . who is the head over *every* power and authority." In Rev. 3:14, "The supervisor *(arche)* of God's creation." In Col. 1:15, "For *by him all things* were created, things in heaven and on earth, visible and invisible." In Mark 14:61–62, "Are you the Christ, the Son of the blessed one? *I am,* said Jesus." In 2 Cor. 5:19, "God was in Christ *reconciling the world* to himself." In John 14:6, *"I am* the way and the truth and the life. *No one* comes to the Father except *through me."* In John 7:17, "If *anyone wills* to do God's will he will *find out* whether my teaching comes from God, or whether I speak on my own."

If we contrast with that the belittling implication that Christ was only a god, do we not at once detect the discord? Does not such a conception conflict with the New Testament message both in whole and in part? Why, if John, in the midst of the idolatry of his day, had made such a statement, would not the first-century hearers and readers have gotten a totally inadequate picture of Christ, who we believe, is the Creator of the universe and the only Redeemer of humanity?

Chapter 30

Is Death the Only
Punishment for Unbelievers?

The claim is made by a few people, chiefly by one sect that contains less than 1 percent of Christendom, that there is no immortality for unbelievers, that their souls perish at the same time that their bodies die. This is a premise assumed and rigidly adhered to, in spite of the fact that Scripture teaches punishment for the unsaved.

It is true that there are a few verses in the New Testament where death is used in a figurative sense. In these passages, death connotes being without the favor and mercy of God, not an end of existence. John wrote that the believer passed from death into life at the time when he accepted Christ (John 5:24). He also stated that the one who does not practice love abides in death (1 John 3:14). Paul, apparently, had a similar idea in mind when he wrote "the wages of sin is death" (Rom. 6:23). At any rate, where the state of the lost is dealt with in detail in the New Testament, punishment after death is specifically mentioned.

Most of us shrink from readily accepting what is taught in the Bible as to the unchangeable destiny and fate of the unredeemed. Especially would we prefer that God's mercy should be extended to them some time in eternity. Since God is motivated by love, will he withhold his forgiveness forever?

However, if the fate of the unsaved is not eternal, we have no statement in the Bible to that effect. But there are many statements to the contrary. Let us read a few of them: "And many of those who sleep in the dust of the earth shall awake, some to everlasting life, and some to shame and everlasting contempt" (Dan. 12:2). "And these will go away into eternal punishment, but the righteous into eternal life" (Matt. 25:46).

In Jehovah's Witnesses' *New World Translation and Kingdom Interlinear Translation* (Matt. 25:46), the Greek word *kolasin,* which is regularly defined punishment in Greek lexicons, is translated "cutting-off," in spite of the fact that there isn't a shred of lexical evidence anywhere for such a translation. We have found this word in first-century Greek writings in 107 different contexts and in every one of them, it has the meaning of punishment, *and never "cutting-off."* But since their premise is that there can be no eternal punishment, they have translated the Scripture to make it somewhat compatible with their theology. By that method, one can easily pervert the biblical teachings and make them teach the opposite of what God intended. Evil can be made to appear good; and black, white. *Kolasin* is also mistranslated *restraint* in 1 John 4:18.

Jesus' vivid, graphic picture of the rich man in torment after death (Luke 16:19–31), certainly teaches retribution for the unsaved, in which account he is informed that he can never escape such punishment since a great impassable gulf separates him in hell from Lazarus in heaven. Here Jesus has drawn back the curtain separating us from eternity and has allowed us to get a glimpse of a man suffering in hell. Here a selfish man is pictured before and after death. If this passage does not teach punishment after death for an unsaved person, what does it teach? Since Lazarus is named in the introduction to the passage, it appears to be not a parable, but rather an account of the different fates of two men who had actually lived on earth. In no biblical parable is a person's name mentioned.

Heb. 9:27, which without any grounds for it in the Greek, is mistranslated in the J.W. Translation—"And as it is reserved for men to die once *for all time,* but after this is a judgment."

But this verse is correctly translated in the R.S.V. "And just as it is appointed for men to die once, and after that comes judgment." Note that the phrase "for all time" was inserted in the former versions without any basis in the original for it. No honest scholar would attempt to so pervert the Word of God! The writer of Hebrews evidently believed that judgment awaited the unredeemed after their death.

The apostle John affirmed the same idea in John 5:29. "The hour is coming when all who are in the tombs will hear his voice and come forth, those who have done good, to the resurrection of life, and those who have done evil, to the resurrection of judgment." Or in other words, death isn't the judgment, but rather, judgment comes after death. Cf. also Heb. 10:27.

The apostle Peter was naive enough also to believe the same. "The Lord knows how to keep the unrighteous under punishment until the day of judgment" (2 Pet. 2:9).

Jesus is quoted to have said the following: "You brood of vipers, how are you to escape being sentenced to hell" (Matt. 23:33). "It is better for you to enter the kingdom of God with one eye than with two eyes to be thrown into hell, where their worm does not die, and the fire is not quenched" (Mark 9:47,48). Cf. also Mark 9:43 and Matt. 13:42, 50. If Jesus did not mean existence in hell after death, why did he say "where their worm does not die"?

Perhaps the chief reason why people do not want to believe in eternal punishment for the unredeemed is due to an inadequate conception of the fact that the New Testament, while teaching that this punishment is to be endless, also teaches that it is not the same for all. Each unbeliever is to suffer according to his misdeeds. In Luke 12:47–48, the statement occurs that some will be punished with few stripes while others, who willfully disobeyed God will be beaten with many stripes. This same teaching of degrees of punishment is reiterated in Rom. 2:5,6: "But by your hard and impenitent heart you are storing up wrath for yourself on the day of wrath when God's righteous judgment will be revealed. For he will render to every man according to his works." God's justice demands that the wicked be requited according to their wickedness. He would not be just, if this were not so. The condition for many will be much more tolerable in hell than it will be for others.

Especially explicit and clear are both the idea of different degrees of punishment and also of its occurrence after death in Rev. 20:12–15: "And the dead were judged out of the things which were written in the books, according to their works. And the sea gave up the dead that were in it, and death and Hades gave up the dead that were in them: and they were judged every man according to their works. And death and Hades were cast into the lake of fire. This is the second death, even the lake of fire. And if any was not found written in the book of life, he was cast into the lake of fire."

Thus, we see that the New Testament teaches that in addition to physical death, there is also for the unsaved a spiritual death, which is identified as the second death and constitutes the eternal penalty for having ignored God and the Lord Jesus Christ. "This is the second death, even the lake of fire."

Chapter 31

The *Reader's Digest* and Mormons

The twenty pages of advertisement in 1979 issues of *Reader's Digest* promoting Mormonism, according to a price list I have, could have cost $1,450,000. What a huge sum for selling cultic anti-Christian religion!

According to the advertisement, Joseph Smith, Jr., at the age of fourteen in 1820, was asking God what church he should join. "A pillar of light, brighter than the sun, descends from heaven. Two personages appear in glory. One points to the other and says, 'This is my beloved Son. Hear Him.' It is the first of several visions of overwhelming impact and authority." It is claimed that, in 1827, an angel helped him find some gold plates with foreign words which, when translated, became the basic part of the Book of Mormon. Some disciples claimed they saw them, but most denied it later on. An angel, it is alleged, took the plates away after the translating was done. They must have been very heavy!

The fourteen-year-old Joseph, when praying, was told, according to the Book of Mormon, that all churches were wrong (quote): "The personage who addressed me said that all their creeds were an abomination in his sight; that those professors (of religion) were all corrupt, and that God would reveal to him the only right way to worship and serve him." According to the above claims, the Mormons have the only correct religion, our Bible has been superseded, and only what agrees with the Book of Mormon is authoritative and inspired. So according to Joe, all Christians face the future without God and hope.

However, Mormons follow only a human being. The Son of God who died for all, will forgive all who trust and *obey him* (John 3:16, 36). They, not we, need to face the future with fear.

There has been a startling *new discovery,* a new book, *Who Really Wrote the Book of Mormon.*[1] Three research historians, Wayne L. Cowdrey, Donald R. Scales, and Howard A. Davis recently made a study of records made by friends and neighbors of Joseph Smith, Jr. and learned, what many have known for years, that Solomon Spalding, a Congregational minister, wrote a novel, *Manuscripts Found,* which was stolen and resurfaced in 1830 as the *Book of Mormon,* with some modifications, which Sidney Rigdon, many thought, had stolen and either gave or sold to Joseph Smith, Jr.

John Spalding, a brother of Solomon, stated "I have recently read the Book of Mormon and to my great surprise I find it nearly the same historical matter, names and so forth as they were in my brother's writings . . . and according to the best of my recollection and belief it is the same as what my brother Solomon wrote." Six other people of that generation made similar statements. Three handwriting specialists have made statements confirming the above records.

Joseph Smith's statement that heavenly visitors told him that "all church creeds were an abomination in his sight." What were these creeds? Beliefs in the teachings of the Bible! Then, in 1827, he said an angel helped him find gold plates, which, when he translated the writing on them, became the Book of Mormon, which is the authoritative guide for Mormons instead of the Bible, which they believe has been miscopied and so is not reliable.

Informed people know that every part of the Bible has been accurately copied, and the translations of today convey the same meanings as the copies of A.D. 30. There are thousands of Bible manuscripts in our libraries. When one copier made a mistake

146

in copying, it was found correct in hundreds of others. So no statement in the Bible has been lost or corrupted.

In 1955, fourteen chapters of the Gospel of John were found in Egypt. It was written near A.D. 150 according to Dr. Bruce Metzger of Princeton, only about sixty years after the apostle John wrote his Gospel. It agrees word for word with the Greek words in my Greek New Testament. Such confirmation is also in other recent discoveries.

Biblical prophets were men of good character. Jesus stated (Matt. 7:15) "Beware of false prophets. . . . You will know them by their fruits." The visit Joseph Smith had with divine beings (?) in 1820, strange to say, did not result in good character; for on March 20, 1826 in Bainbridge, New York, he was tried in court and found guilty of having used fraudulent means to obtain money from Mr. Bridgeman. Years later, while living in Missouri, he spent some time in prisons in Jackson County and in Liberty in Clay County. (I have seen the prison in Liberty.) He was incarcerated on the grounds of stealing cattle, I was informed. "In 1838 the Governor of Missouri issued an exterminating order against the Latter Day Saints, and they were driven out of the state. They went to Illinois, where by 1840 . . . they had founded the city of Nauvoo." An article in the local newspaper accused "the prophet" to be guilty of "immoralities and misdeeds." He had the printing office destroyed. For this, he was arrested on orders from the governor. On June 27, 1844, a mob attacked the jail and killed him. (Data in *Colliers Encyclopedia,* page 309.)

Did God "fire" Jesus Christ and nominate and appoint Joseph Smith, Jr. as his successor? Did Joseph Smith, Jr. have angels welcome his birth with singing when he was born: Did he go about "doing good" as Jesus did? What miracles did he perform? Did he ever raise anyone from the dead as Jesus did? He did not rise from the dead, as Jesus did, and spend forty days visiting with his disciples. He did not ascend visibly "into heaven" as Jesus did. "This Jesus who was taken up from you into heaven, will come in the same way as you saw him go into heaven" (Acts 1:11).

147

"I am the way, the truth and the life. *No one* comes to the Father except through me" (John 14:6).

"He who rejects me and does not receive *my teachings* has one judging him, the word which *I* have spoken. *That* will judge him *in the last day*" (John 12:48).

Note

1. Wayne L. Cowdrey, Donald R. Scales, and Howard A. Davis, *Who Really Wrote the Book of Mormon?* Santa Ana, CA: Vision House Publishers, 1978.

Chapter 32

Baptized for the Dead

Chapter 15 of 1 Corinthians deals primarily with the resurrection of Christ, the resurrection of the dead, and the resurrection of the body. The statement in most translations in verse 28 "the Son himself will be subjected to him" (God), should read "will subject *himself* to him." For the verb is middle in form in Greek, not passive.

As to the next verse (29), the Mormons claim (*Reader's Digest,* October 1979) that they can save some of their dead relatives by being baptized for them. This verse is their authority for it, I believe. "What will those do that are being baptized for the dead?"

There is no statement anyplace else in the New Testament nor in early church history that a Christian can save another person by being baptized for him, alive or dead.

The Greek preposition *uper* (for), with the genitive case, occurs 148 times in the Greek New Testament. It does mean 'for' frequently. But according to the contexts, it has other meanings, one of which is 'because of,' in 1 Cor. 10:30 (in NIV); 2 Cor. 1:11; 5:12; 7:4; 12:8; Gal. 1:4; 2 Thess. 1:4; 1 Peter 3:19, "Christ died because of your sins to bring you to God." Both the Liddell and Scott and the Arndt-Gingrich lexicons give 'because of' as one of the meanings of *uper*.

People were accepting Christ and joining churches by baptism because they wanted, when Christ returns to earth, to receive new bodies for living on the renewed earth (Rom. 8).

Baptism does not save one, according to the New Testament. It is commanded and is one act of obedience. It is evidence that one has decided to join Christ's crowd and live in full accordance with his will the rest of life. Can anything be nobler than that? America and the world are in desperate need for citizens of that type, who are honest, unselfish, loving, forgiving, moral, generous, and always dependable. They are the best type of citizens and neighbors. We all love such.

"For by *grace* you have been saved through faith; and this is not your own doing, it is *the gift of God*—not because of works, lest any man should boast. For we are *his workmanship, created* by Christ Jesus *for good works*" (Eph. 2:8–10).

Mormons believe their good deeds and their organization save them. That is Noah's Ark religion, not Christianity.

Chapter 33

Too Good to Be True!

But Charles Colson, former "hatchet man" attorney for President Nixon, and who spent several months in a federal prison, says it is true. He became a Christian before imprisonment; and after release organized "prison fellowship." All his royalties from the movie *Born Again,* are spent helping prisoners. Not only does he and other ex-prisoners conduct week-long Christian seminars in prisons, but he is also getting remarkable cooperation from Christians outside prison walls, who on a one-to-one basis became pen pals with prisoners. for example, "A few weeks ago, I was in Canon City, Colorado, one of the toughest, most overcrowded institutions in America. Following our service in the packed chapel, a young inmate, his eyes sparkling, caught my arm. 'Thank you, Mr. Colson, thank you,' he kept repeating. 'I have been in this prison eight years. No one has ever visited or written to me.'

" 'Six months ago,' he continued, 'I wrote you and asked for a Pen Pal. I want you to know that I have hope now for the first time in my life.' "

Also, splendid cooperation is coming from church members near prisons who conduct regular services in the prisons in their areas.

Another example: "In the largest walled prison in the world,

Jackson, Michigan, 125 men attended our week-long seminar, that was the beginning, like the striking of a spark. The fellowship has grown with each passing week in size and strength. Hundreds of Christians in the community volunteered. Recently, prison officials asked us to assume the responsibility for continuing teaching programs and ministry inside.''

What are some outstanding results?

''More than 200 inmates of about 40 prisons (2 from each prison) across the country have gone through the out-of-prison training periods (2 weeks) and are back inside, continuing the work.'' Colson said none of the temporarily released prisoners ever has betrayed the trust in them.

''It's a miracle it hasn't happened,'' he said. ''We expected occasional problems or incidents, but there haven't been any.''

Colson says, ''the prison system is an abysmal failure. The prisons are not working. They are not rehabilitative. They've got to be radically reformed.''

He says, ''Four out of five ex-convicts return to crime again. But in contrast not even one of genuinely converted criminals does.'' How amazing! If it's true.

He also has said that it costs about $20,000 a year per prisoner. What a saving to taxpayers when thousands are converted! When released and employed again, they are not only exemplary citizens, but are taxpayers as well. Instead of being dangerous and a debit, they become assets in society.

George W. Cornell, in an Associated Press article, recently quoted Colson as saying, ''It's up to Christians if anything is ever going to be done about changes in the prisons. No one else really cares.''

The apostle Paul wrote, ''If anyone is in Christ, he is a new creature; the old has passed away, behold! All has become new'' (2 Cor. 5:17).

Jesus said, to be so motivated, ''You must be born again'' (John 3:7). That is called regeneration. To experience it; ''Not everyone who says to me, Lord, Lord, will enter the Kingdom of heaven, but only he *who does the will* of my Father who is in heaven'' (Matt. 7:21). ''Whoever believes in the Son has eternal life. But whoever disobeys the Son will not see that life, for God's wrath remains on him" (John 3:36).

Other verses also state the same truth: "If you confess with your mouth, 'Jesus is Lord,' and believe in your heart that God raised him from the dead, you will be saved" (Rom. 10:9). "Repent and be baptized, *everyone of you,* in the name of Jesus Christ, for the forgiveness of sins, and you will receive the *gift* of the *Holy Spirit* . . . whom God gave to those that obeyed him" (Acts 2:38; 5:32).

Ten years ago, Art Linkletter's daughter jumped to her death, apparently during an LSD trip. Since then, he has been majoring in helping young people escape from drugs. He said a few days ago. "I've sat in halfway houses with kids so far gone, you'd think it is hopeless. But I've found that no life is so broken God can't repair it." He said those who had accepted Christ were insulated against disappointments that bring on drug use. "They have a relationship that makes Jesus Christ available on a hotline 24 hours a day."

Since the first of this year, there has been a 15 percent increase in crime in the United States. Our prisons are too small, so judges are paroling many prisoners to make room for new ones, most of whom commit new crimes.

One of every three marriages of unbelievers end in divorce. But only one in ten does when both are born-again Christians.

How valuable is the gift of the Spirit? It enriches one's life beyond all earth's treasures! It means that God has come into your life, that you have been born again (John 3:7), that you have been exalted into a heavenly and extraordinary dimension of living in which joy, love, self-control, and self-respect are experienced as never before. It means pardon for the past, peace for the present, and assurance, hope, and security for all eternity.

Can anyone afford to be without this fantastic and eternal gift? I would rather lose all my possessions, health, mind, friends, loved ones, everything than that.

If parents want their children to have good character and the respect of others, the best way is to have them regularly attend worship services and to become friends of God-fearing companions. "Bad company corrupts good character" (1 Cor. 15:33).